M D Dawkins

PATTERNS FOR SELF-UNFOLDMENT

by

Randolph and Leddy Schmelig

UNITY BOOKS • UNITY VILLAGE, MO.

LLC: 74-29429
ISBN: 0-87159-127-8

CONTENTS

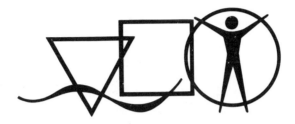

Lowell Turner, who created this design symbolizing "Patterns for Self-Unfoldment," explains it in these words:

The wave represents the ups and downs of life—simply, the problem of apparent good and evil. It is lower in the design, but prominent enough to say that we must become aware of suffering to the point of sincere questioning.

The triangle represents spiritual thought or concern for heavenly things, one of which typically is the trinity.

The square represents the presence of external nature in our mind, or concern for the world (the vehicle or raft of the Spirit).

The circle represents spiritual realization: universal love, unity, oneness.

The human figure represents the freedom experienced in spiritual realization. (The figure's right arm and hand stretch out of the circle to stabilize the world.)

Finally, all the parts are tied together to show how the patterns indeed fit together—that out of chaos (wave) can come equilibrium (triangle), and out of equilibrium comes security (square), a good state; and out of these comes spiritual realization, the ultimate outcome. These are the basic patterns, yet there are many patterns (many lessons) within these.

Pattern One

Lesson 1

Dear Student:

You are now beginning the most thrilling adventure of your life. You are setting out today to discover that things are not really as they seem—that life is not what you may have thought it to be, but infinitely more wonderful!

Here are patterns for self-unfoldment that can serve to guide and uplift you in this great adventure. These patterns of thought, feeling, and action are meant not only to clarify the many-faceted process of spiritual development, but also to indicate, to praise, and gratefully to acknowledge the ever-outward expanding, the continually-upward spiraling unfoldment that is now taking place in you.

These ideas are basics; you will see at once that they are simple and familiar. You have probably heard the same ideas dozens of times before. Yet you know, too, that somehow they cannot be told enough or in enough different ways. There is in you a perpetual longing and recognition that never tires of these basics. These simple ideas are the prerequisites for all beginners, and they are the requirements for each advancing seeker. The call is always the same—the basics are always the same, after all.

If these fundamentals should seem to become tiresome, then the essence of them has been lost track of somehow. The eternal joy and infinite blessing of them are still there to be rediscovered. It is impossible to pray too often, or to start at the very foundations of things too often. For these simple ideas are the life of life, the stuff of all religion and philosophy, the recurrent theme of all knowledge; they are really the pulse of every single moment in every single day forever. If there are times of dryness in life, then these basics are the answers; they are the unfailing refreshment for all.

More complex systems of thought only

repeat these same beginnings over and over again. It is necessary to abandon the belief that there is a "higher philosophy." There is no higher philosophy than what shines within you at this moment as "simple" and "basic." There is no higher philosophy than the starting point of all philosophy, and that is the realization that your real nature and the real nature of each person is spiritual; and that the true source of happiness and fulfillment is somehow back of appearances, more permanent and more real than changing circumstances can generate; and that the flux of all things is spiritual, eternal, all-pervasive, One.

You know that you are unfolding toward this realization now and always. Keep this perception kindled, for it is the very foundation of all understanding.

In this series of lessons, you will not be studying metaphysical semantics or scientific explanations. This is not a course in dogma or doctrine, but a pattern for a new and dynamic personal experience.

Every scientific invention that has ever come about, every business that has ever been established, every religious movement or philosophy that has ever been formulated has stemmed more or less dramatically from someone's idea, someone's personal experience.

The common attribute of all religions and philosophies is that each of their founders and forerunners has experienced a magnificent idea, a flash of insight, a spiritual communion with God, that transformed his life and the lives of those he touched.

The containment of these grand experiences into doctrines and terminology has always been a secondary activity. The forms and phrases of organized religion alone have never been able completely to transport students of religion to that grand experience itself. Somehow, after the idea is codified it becomes simply a second- or third-hand report. Something is missing—the experience itself.

You have already read and reread second- and third-hand reports about God, Divine Mind, the Creator, or whatever term suits your concept of divinity. You have looked everywhere for the answers to your questions. By now you know that words alone will not give you the key to true peace and happiness;

you seek the *experience.*

In the lives of saints and sages, a great deal of mental and physical work seems to have preceded a transforming experience. Each "prepared the way" through concentrated effort and thought. By undertaking this course of study, you have taken the first step already: you have decided to consciously acknowledge and work with your own unfoldment in this way. Through your attitude of determination and receptiveness, you are preparing the way for the experience you seek.

You are preparing yourself for a new understanding of life that will illumine the "dark corners" of your mind and light your way from daydreams to reality. The light of understanding is ever shining within you as the part of you that is one with God. But as the sun, though constantly shining, may be temporarily eclipsed, so you may stand in your own way and allow a limited viewpoint to hide much of the truth about yourself. Still, a "glimmer" of that true Self shines around the shadowy edges of the mind. As you learn to look for it, more and more of this understanding shines into your life and you stand in fuller awareness of the limitless potential that is within you.

Through this illumined understanding, you look at the world more keenly and see that there are miracles everywhere! A world of apparent lack and darkness is revealed to be a world of plenty and light.

You feel your body infused with a new energy; your every cell and system revitalized. All that you undertake is blessed, the good you receive is multiplied, and the individuals you meet are drawn to you by the freeing, harmonizing power of God's love.

But truly the greatest blessing of all is the inexpressible *first-hand* experience of God that awaits you. You will find God in your own unique way by preparing the way in your mind and heart. *You will know God for yourself as He has never been known before.*

God has led you to this series of lessons, and He will guide you to a great new experience through it. Hold no thought but that you will succeed. All that is needed is for you to hold firm to that guidance. Resolve to get the very best from your practice; be zealous and courageous in your pursuit. Although the work may seem hard and demanding at times, and the obstacles many and difficult, remember that the reward is wonderful beyond measure and that, in reality, the goal is at hand.

As you meet new challenges and make new discoveries during your studies, know that you are never alone, but that you are united with all other students of Truth in a constant, loving bond of prayer.

Guidelines for Practice

1. *An attitude of expectancy*

All along you have suspected that life holds a promise for you—a promise of joyous fulfillment beyond all expectations. Now at last you may begin to *expect* all your dreams to become manifest! The first requirement for successful practice is an attitude of *expectancy*. Know that you are on the very brink of a terrific realization; you need merely prepare the way by letting old beliefs of fear and limitation slip away. You need no longer accept a second- or third-hand report about God—you now seek a *direct realization*. Open your mind to the infinite possibilities that await you. Expect a miracle every moment!

2. *Thankfulness*

As you read each new lesson, make a habit of thanking God for the great opportunity it represents, and for the divine potential within you that enables you to realize boundless dividends through it. Recognize God within you as your Teacher, and open your mind to receive His inspiration. Do not be concerned with *how* your study activities are working to help you, and do not worry about whether results will come immediately. Simply know that if you practice and study faithfully *wonderful results are certain!*

3. *Willingness and readiness*

Your success depends on two other very important conditions: your *willingness* and your *readiness.* These two conditions are interdependent; you know that if you are truly willing to begin this search for a new understanding, you also feel ready and able to work at it. If you have a sincere desire to transform your life, you must be ready to place this goal foremost in your mind. Have no doubts about your capability—the only way to become capable is simply to *begin.*

4. *Study and practice plan*

On the day you begin the course, read and study Lesson 1 of Pattern One entirely and follow the suggestions in the Practice Exercise at the close of the material. For a period of one week, reread the Practice Exercise section and use your imagination as it suggests in each daily study time. During the week, you may wish to refer to the material in Lesson 1 to refresh your memory and redirect your thinking. At the end of a week's study and practice, you will be ready to go on to Lesson 2. Follow the same procedure with each lesson. In this way, each lesson of the four-part Patterns will require one week of study and practice. Be sure to study and use each lesson for a full week before beginning the next lesson. You will find that in this way, you will derive the fullest benefit and understanding from each lesson, and you will progress easily and naturally.

At the first reading, these lessons may seem very simple. It is true that these principles are simple, although not necessarily easy to apply consistently. The simple things in life are often the most difficult, and the most neglected. In practice, you will find how challenging the task can be of controlling the mind and constructively directing the imagination.

5. *Daily practice*

You will get great benefit from your studies if you will endeavor to devote approximately fifteen minutes each day to mental exercise. Choose a time when it is most convenient for you to practice. If you choose the morning, be sure to get up early enough so that you have plenty of time before you begin the rest of your daily routine. If you choose the afternoon, be sure that you are able to put aside all interferences long enough to complete your course work. If the evening is the most convenient time for you, plan to allow sufficient time for practice so that you will still be assured of having the right amount of sleep. Whatever time of day you choose, plan to practice at the *same time each day*.

6. *Choosing a place to practice*

You will discover that your work will be especially meaningful if you choose a regular place to practice your exercises. A quiet place, removed from distractions, is the best

16

setting. You may prefer a comfortable chair in your bedroom; you may find that the peaceful atmosphere that this activity brings to the room will help make your sleep more restful, and that you will look forward to awakening each morning in a room you have blessed with many hours of prayer and creative thought. Whatever area you choose, it is best that you find some place to practice where you may be alone and undisturbed.

7. *Physical preparation for practice*

You will also find it easier to practice if you have allowed time for digestion after a meal. Then you will be more able to focus all your physical as well as mental energy on this activity. Controlling the mind is a very delicate undertaking, and you will want to give your whole attention to the work at hand. Be comfortable when you study, but *be at attention.* Your good physical posture should grow into a good mental posture. Learn to feel your body perfectly balanced; at ease, yet completely attentive to your mental attitude. As your mind and body become still, nothing will disturb you from within or from without.

8. *Mental preparation for practice*

Learn to set aside the cares of the day when you begin your practice. You will find that when your exercise is over, the problems that concerned you before have been translated by a new understanding, and are already on the way to being solved. Your practice time is not a *recess* from productive activity, but the time of your *most productive activity,* of your *greatest achievement.*

9. *Self-discipline*

You will find as you continue that although daily practice may at times seem difficult or frustrating, if you diligently exercise your thinking every day, the experience you will gain will soon transmute what once may have seemed a duty to an activity of love. You will find yourself looking forward to your exercise each day, and you will eagerly await each new lesson as you feel the dramatic freeing effects of your practice.

Once you realize that the old way of thinking provides no escape from the endless routine, then you know that the only way to go is *up!* Release from limitations is attained by rising out of a limiting attitude into the sunlight of a higher approach. The climb will be demanding; you will need serious commitment and self-discipline. But you will persevere because of your great desire. Through the power and wisdom available to you through God within you, all goals are attained, all questions are answered, all things are made possible.

10. *Affirmation*

Holding steadfast in your mind or speaking aloud statements of Truth (affirmations), you make definite, positive suggestions to your mind. In this way, you express your power to know the Truth about yourself. All of your thoughts contribute to the general trend of your thinking, which in turn determines the quality and direction of your life. By affirming what is true, even in the face of contrary appearances, you exercise your power of will to readjust your attitudes, and thus to change your life. You actively prepare your mind really to experience the Truth about life. In an attitude of zeal and enthusiasm, take a deep breath and affirm for yourself: *I am open and receptive to God's infinite possibilities for me. I am willing and ready to seek my highest good.* Keep this attitude of mind as you begin your first lesson.

Get ready for a new experience!

SPIRITUAL DIARY

It has been found that recording personal experiences and ideas relating to the course material is both a helpful and an inspiring activity. In reality, this "learning activity" is not a matter of "input"—it is not something that is fed into you; rather, true development is really a matter of "output"—the uncovering and showing forth of that which is already shining within you. Your inner potential is unfolding in a tremendous, many-faceted way. Therefore, keep notes always—keep a constant interest, a constant watch on your own spiritual growth. You will be thrilled to learn so much of yourself; and you will be blessed and uplifted to learn so infinitely much *through* yourself.

By keeping this Spiritual Diary, you constantly bless this material, and through it you are blessed in return. Let these lessons be augmented, strengthened, and enriched by your own unique and special perception of

Truth. Keep a notebook of your own throughout your study of these lessons, and continually add your individual insight and understanding to the material. A school-size, three-ring looseleaf notebook would be good for this purpose.

In this way, it will be easy to add your own notes at various times and in various places in the notebook. Include in your writings not only rephrasings of the lesson material for your own understanding, but also thoughts and feelings you have during your studies that may not on the surface appear to relate directly to the lesson. When you look back on these valuable notes, you will see a living story of growth and spiritual unfoldment that no objective testing could provide.

Throughout this course, you will be reminded to keep your Spiritual Diary, and you will be given helpful suggestions to direct your note-taking. Remember that your personal commitment and involvement in this endeavor is the secret of your success. You yourself are the center of this great, ever evolving pattern of unfoldment!

PATTERN ONE

Learning to Let Go

Lesson 1: Taking Time

You are about to begin an important experiment; your hypothesis is that there is a positive, spiritual way of life that is also immanently practical. Your aim is to *get results* that verify this hypothesis in your own life. You no longer seek theories about the experience—you are ready for the experience itself.

Just as a scientist sees that his laboratory is clean and in order before he sets up his equipment for an experiment, you must put yourself in order; you must clear your physical and mental "laboratory" of all extraneous material. You must relax and let go of all extraneous cares and concerns during your study time. You have accepted the challenge of seeking the very highest, the very best experience, so you must bring to your study only *your* highest and best thoughts and attitudes.

As you enter the room you have chosen for your study, consciously leave all thoughts and worries outside. As you cross the threshold, you are crossing into a new experience—one in which there is no room for worry or limitation.

Just as a scientist would select and sterilize his equipment very carefully for an experiment, so you must choose and bless your materials. You must mentally cleanse your mental and physical setting in preparation for perfect results.

As you sit in the chair you have chosen for study, think how peaceful and comfortable it is. As you think thoughts of praise about it, say:

I consecrate and dedicate this place in God's name.

By affirming this idea, you will feel instantly lifted out of the everyday as you sit in your special place. Close your eyes for a moment and repeat the words:

I consecrate and dedicate this place in God's name.

Each time you sit in this chair, you will feel this blessing, this positive thought in action, helping you mentally and physically to prepare the way for something wonderful to happen.

In the same way that the place you have chosen for study is sanctified and blessed by your thinking about it, the period of time you decide to set aside each day for your study is also a "holy time."

Some days you may feel that you have finished your study within the fifteen-minute period you have set aside; or you may find the time you need for study stretches beyond that limit as you progress in the course. Whatever amount of time may be needed for you to gain the desired results, discipline yourself to maintain the *minimum* fifteen-minute study period. Yet you must also use your will to deny false ideas about time as a depressing restriction on your activity. The following definition may help you to reach a fuller understanding about the idea of time.

time—The limitation of man's consciousness of space. A day is a measure of time in the realm of effects. A sidereal day is that period in which the earth rotates once on its axis. Man divided that period into seconds, minutes, hours, and thus invented time.

Time is the measure that man gives to passing events. The only power in time is what man imparts to it. When man gets into the understanding of the Absolute, he takes his freedom from all bondage of time and declares that time shall no more enter into the substance of his mind or body or affairs *(Charles Fillmore, The Revealing Word).*

Read the second paragraph of this passage once more, and think of it in relation to yourself. Affirm this statement:

I declare my freedom from all bondage of time;

The time I use is consecrated and dedicated in God's name.

Now close your eyes for a moment. Let the papers fall to your lap. Close out completely all conception of time as a hindrance to you. As you repeat once again the affirmation above, and as you accept the truth of the words, truly *you* are consecrated and dedicated in God's name!

What a thrilling idea that is—to be *consecrated and dedicated in God's name!* You need to longer think of yourself as dedicated to any time limits. You are no longer dedicated to hurrying to finish your work, hurrying to eat, hurrying to sleep, hurrying to live.

You are now consecrated and dedicated in God's name, and you are heir to all eternity.

So many times you may have said to yourself: "Not now, I'm too busy. Perhaps later, or tomorrow, or next week, or next year I will have time to settle down to look, to listen, to study, to think, to pray. But right now, I just don't have the time to spare." In these periods, you probably have found that you were not really achieving anything, but were simply "spinning your wheels." You know from experience that hurrying through life is self-limiting. The truth is that you have all the time in the world when you decide to live in the eternal *now*.

Everything good that has ever happened to you has happened when for a moment or a day or a week, you forgot about time, and just enjoyed life. There is within you something which perceives that God's gift of time is infinite. Through that perception within you, you forget easily about time when something stimulates your imagination or interest or when you are with people you love—whenever something wonderful is happening. Time limits fall away from your mind, and you begin to understand the truth about life.

When you are in tune with that understanding, you know that you do not need to wait for a particular situation or possession to come to you, but that happiness can come in an *instant,* wisdom in a *flash;* peace can be yours *right now.* All you need to do is prepare the way in your thinking for this realization.

Let yesterday go, and let tomorrow go. Hold to each moment of the *now,* for within it is the treasure of all greatness and all joy. Now is the time to know the Truth.

As you realize this truth, you will understand how the world can be changed in fifteen minutes, or in one minute. For time means nothing in relation to Truth.* " 'Ye shall know the truth, and the truth shall make you free'—and there is no time limit to the promise. Whether 'God's instant' be a second or a century depends on our individual application of Truth" *(James A. Decker, Magnificent Decision).*

*Truth may be defined as "that which is, has been, and ever will be; that which eternally is. The Truth of God is reality: 'the same yesterday and today, *yea* and

27

for ever.' The verities of being are eternal and have always existed. Truth abides in fullness at the very core of man's being. As his consciousness (awareness) expands, he touches the everlasting Truth. What seems new is but the unveiling of that which has always been" *(Charles Fillmore, The Revealing Word).*

Reread both of these quotes several times, until you are able to get into the feeling of the ideas expressed. Then proceed to the Practice Exercise.

Practice Exercise

To use time rightly is to take with you always the thought that you live and move in God's good time. As you relax your body in a comfortable but attentive position, let your mind become more and more receptive to this idea. Through affirmation, firmly suggest the idea to your mind by saying:

I live and move in God's good time.

As your mind opens to this idea, imagine that you are walking down a road that stretches out behind you into infinity, and stretches out before you into infinity. The scenery along the road is amazingly beautiful, and you have *all the time in the world* to enjoy it.

Now close your eyes for a moment and mentally walk down this beautiful road. Remember that there is no need to hurry, for you are free of the bondage of time.

If you have any difficulty at all envisioning this thought, pause for a moment, breathe deeply. Then repeat the affirmation and let your mind dwell on the ideas in this material. Close your eyes and your thoughts to outside disturbances, and easily and peacefully form your own mental picture of the road.

Each day as you continue to exercise your

creative imagination in this way, work with the image until you can picture it readily and naturally. It will become a vivid reminder that in reality, today and every day, eternity is yours.

As you carry this thought with you, consciously slow your pace while walking or driving. You will find that you get so much more out of life each day by letting go of the belief that time is a restriction on your life and affairs and by consciously accepting God's infinite gift of time. All things that need to be done will be done in perfect order, in perfect time. If ever you feel the impulse to rush through an experience, remind yourself of the ideas you have been studying. Resist tension and hurry by mentally transporting yourself for just a moment to that beautiful road in your thoughts and repeat silently to yourself:

I live and move in God's good time.

If you feel the temptation to become annoyed by someone who may seem to be detaining you by not moving quickly enough, bless this individual by silently affirming:

You live and move in God's good time.

As you find wonderful results of this exercise happening to you, make note of these experiences in your Spiritual Diary. You will find that constantly living in God's good time brings order and peace to your affairs and to the affairs of those around you.

You may wish to record in your Spiritual Diary your own impressions and ideas about such questions as these:

What is my own concept of time?

What are my feelings regarding my place of study?

How do I personally determine whether or not something is true?

Does my criterion fit in with the definition of Truth given in this lesson?

How has my expanded idea of time affected my own daily schedule?

In what ways am I now unfolding?

Pattern One
Lesson 2

Dear Student:

Give thanks, for you are blessed! You are discovering for yourself that in life, *experience is the thing.* What freedom, what joy, what victory lies in experience! Here, and here alone, true growth and true fulfillment await you.

As you think about the many experiences you have, you begin to realize that experience appears to have two main phases or aspects. There is activity—change and movement of some kind—in experience; there is a constant interplay of cause and effect. And too, there is a part of you, a phase of experience itself, that quietly watches in utter stillness, observing all that is occurring and translating experiences into eternal lessons of Truth.

In both ways you take part in, enact, observe, and value experience. You are both active and passive, both in and out of the game. You are engaged in a quiet activity as well as in an active quietness. For you know you are both ever changing and yet innately changeless; inwardly immovable, yet also endlessly in motion.

You are really always expressing what seems to be the very character of yourself, of nature, of life, and of God—the dual nature of active change and of changelessness, that which is beyond action.

The secret of happiness lies in the discovery of a kind of "rhythm" within this apparently dual nature. To realize true peace, harmony, and stillness, you must actively—even vigorously—seek this realization. At the same time, in order to discover meaningful activity, in order to express the realization dynamically, it is necessary to learn true stillness. Ultimately you find that a perpetual harmony exists between the two.

In order to be aware of both processes—both views of the same unfoldment—at once, begin to be attentive to the idea of rhythm in all that you experience. There are "ups and downs" in life; there are periods of relative activity and times of relative stillness in your body, in your emotions, in your thinking, in your unfoldment, as well as in all that surrounds you. As you become more in tune with this universal rhythm, you find a new peace *and* a new energy. You attain a great sense of stability, and at the same time, a boundless freedom.

Dwell on the idea of this divine rhythm and joyously look forward to great experience as you undertake this lesson. Remember always that you are divinely sustained and guided in all that you do, for you are enfolded by infinite love and directed by divine wisdom.

PATTERN ONE

Learning to Let Go

Lesson 2: Mental Music

The concept of time as a negative limit typifies a common misunderstanding about man's relationship to the universe. In believing that time is an inescapable limit, man has mistakenly accepted the concept that he is a slave to the universe of appearances and believes himself to be in perpetual bondage. By holding to this belief he ignores the elastic properties of thought. He forgets that through the power of God moving through the human mind, a minute can be expanded to eternity; eternity can be contracted to the blink of an eye.

Last week you began to stretch your mind beyond the limits of time. You are discovering that your quest for a spiritual experience is not necessarily on a "weekly schedule," but that every moment holds an eternity of possibilities. Somewhere between one second and the next, an idea may come that will really *change your mind* from a limiting belief to a freeing realization. In a period of a few weeks or months an attitude may be slowly evolving to redirect your life completely. The "time involved" in an experience is no longer a consideration, for in real spiritual and mental progress, "time" is not really involved at all.

However, holding to the concept of time has provided a sense of security, of order. It has been easy to place yourself in a context of time, to sequence all your activities within the confines of hours and days and weeks and months. But now you have begun to reverse the situation. You are learning to place time in a context of *your own experience.* You began by fantasizing about an endless road. The fantasy became a tool to a real experience of timelessness. Once you gained this experience, the idea of time that once seemed so real became unreal and irrelevant to your experience. What was once a fantasy began to reveal a truth about yourself.

You now know that something within you is eternal, unbound by time. Thinking about freedom from time seems natural and pleasing to that part of you. Something in you *corresponds to eternity.* Know for yourself:

I am unbound by time. I am eternal, free spirit.

By affirming this idea, you affirm your oneness with God, your unity with all creation. "Spirit, our innermost, real being, the absolute part of us, the *I* of us, has never changed, though our thoughts and our circumstances may have changed hundreds of times. This part of us is a standing forth of God into visibility. It is the Father in us. At this central part of his being every person can say, 'I and the Father are one,' and speak absolute Truth" *(H. Emilie Cady, Lessons in Truth).*

You now begin to perceive your true relationship to God and the universe. You begin to experience an order and security beyond the old, limited concept of time. You begin to feel a pervading rhythm and balance that supersedes appearances.

You have learned mentally to *stop* time, to lift yourself out of a limited context to a new perspective. You are beginning to look more closely at the beauty of the world as you take time to enjoy your surroundings. Now you must begin to *listen* very carefully for a new experience.

Through the ability to change your mental perspective, you have the power to shift your attention from tension and confusion in life to that center of peace and harmony, that unbound, free spirit that is your true self. You can transport your thinking beyond the apparent disharmony of a situation by thinking about that part of you which is naturally in harmony with the universe.

Read the following paragraph carefully; try to get an idea of the kind of experience the writer describes.

"To keep himself in tune with the great divine harmony of life is the most important business of man. Above the strife and din of existence, there is always the eternal, heavenly symphony. At any time, under any circumstance, we can feel the peace of its divine melody. It is here just as the air is here. All that is required of us to enter into its sweet harmony is that we open our mind and heart and find the joy and peace that we so much desire" *(May Rowland, Dare to Believe!)*

Remember, keeping in tune with "the great divine harmony of life" is your *most important business.* The experience of being in harmony with all of life is not replaceable by any legacy of wealth, by any position of authority, by any university degree. This harmony, this oneness with life, must be your first concern.

You may have to face a great mental struggle to remind yourself in *all circumstances* that this harmony is immediately available to you, that it is always here, "just as the air is here." It seems easier to think of harmony as an abstract principle, as something separate and perfect, removed from life here and now.

Harmony may be defined as "perfect accord with the goodness, the beauty, and the righteousness of omnipresent Spirit" *(Charles Fillmore, The Revealing Word).* Such perfect harmony may seem to exist only in an imaginary world—a place far distant in time and place. Harmony seems to be like the ending in an old movie; the lovers embrace in the sunset as violins play dreamily in the background.

But the musical background has really been there all along, even during the struggle and the suspense. At those times, however, your mind was on the action taking place. You were caught up in the drama.

Right now, your mind may be caught up in the drama, the struggle and suspense of your own life. To have an awareness of harmony, you must look away from the drama and listen very carefully for the background of musical unity, of harmony in life. You have already discovered that you have a natural inclination for the finer side of existence, for the truth about yourself. Follow that inclination. Turn your thoughts within, away from apparent disharmony and confusion, away from fear and lack, away from disease and discord. Be still for a moment and listen within.

"The spirit of music is within all of us. When we have developed and brought it forth . . . then we will realize that there is a power in us which will produce harmony. . . .

"Thinking in wisdom produces harmony of mind and grace of body. All discord is produced by ignorant, unwise thoughts and words" *(Charles Fillmore, Dynamics for Living).*

As you reread the passage above, you will discover more and more what a rich source of ideas it is. You will begin to discover that harmony is not something distant and abstract, but something real and immediate.

Practice Exercise

Relax your body and your mind as you sit in your study area, and turn your attention away from any worries or distractions in your thoughts. Remember that this place is a "holy place," consecrated and dedicated in God's name. All thoughts of confusion are out of place here. Consciously banish discord from your mind and turn your thoughts within to receive a new and fulfilling experience.

Think of a beautiful tune that soothes your mind and brings pleasant thoughts. As you remember this tune, you can almost hear the music playing in your mind. Concentrate on the music; feel it filling the very air around you. As you listen within, you can hear each instrument playing in perfect pitch and rhythm. All of the players are playing together; all of your thoughts are in perfect harmony.

You feel all tension slip away from you, and you are filled with the music. The sounds that surround you in the room, the quiet rustle of your papers, and the small sounds of your breathing are all brought together in the tune. All things, inside and out, are in harmonious unity. Affirm:

I am in tune with the infinite . . .

I am filled with God's rhythm and harmony.

As the music inspires and relaxes you, all thoughts of inharmony and confusion slip away; you feel a new freedom and balance. Let your body sway slightly with this "mental music." Feel the tune harmonizing all your

41

body systems, filling every cell with vibrant health.

As you listen within, your breathing becomes regular and rhythmic. Your entire body is like a musical instrument, receiving and responding to the inspiration of God.

Now you will begin to feel the influence of this idea of music in your movements, in your speech, and in your thoughts and feelings. The awareness of harmony in and through life will reflect in harmonious thinking, grace and greater ease of movement, and a general revitalization of your entire body.

As you feel yourself more and more in tune with God within you, you begin to know more fully for yourself

I am filled with God's rhythm and harmony,

He sings His song through me.

Prepare your mind to take this idea with you as you leave your study place. Know that God's rhythm and harmony *are* at work to bring order and peace to your life inside and out. Every day you will feel more in harmony with life in every way.

Each time you are confronted with a tense situation, each time you feel discord or disunity threatening your peace of mind, remember your "mental music." Focus your thoughts on the harmony of the tune in your thoughts. Repeat for yourself the affirmations in this exercise, and know for everyone you meet:

You are filled with God's rhythm and harmony,

He sings His song through you.

If you will deliberately focus your mind on these ideas of harmony, you will find that your mental "musical background" will carry you through the struggles and the suspense of life; your mind will no longer be caught up in the drama, it will be concentrated and poised in the underlying background of harmony that pervades all things.

Return to your study place each day and direct your mind to this exercise. First read it carefully and slowly, letting your mind follow the suggestions in the exercise. Then close your eyes and listen to the music within you. Let your thoughts dwell on its harmonizing, life-giving influence.

Do not neglect your Spiritual Diary as you grow and learn in these experiences. Be sure to include your impressions and special insights as you consider such questions as these:

At what times in my life have I felt the most in harmony?

How has the new sense of mental harmony I am discovering affected my trend of thinking and reacting day to day?

In what ways am I now unfolding?

Pattern One
Lesson 3

Dear Student:

Greetings of love and joy flow out to you as you seek and find a harmony in life that transcends and translates appearances! Regardless of the confusion that may seem to exist at times in the world, the hint keeps coming back to you: "There is an eternal stability, an ultimate fulfillment, an unshakable peace behind and through everything, and I can reach it somehow! There is something I can count on—I feel it, and I will realize it!" Rely always on that inner knowing, that inner certainty, and follow this leading to ever greater unfoldment.

In the preceding lesson you affirmed, *"I am eternal, free Spirit."* If you are serious and thoughtful as you affirm this statement, various impressions come to the mind that are significant. Perhaps there is a slight sense of being somewhat startled as you first encounter the idea. It is understandable that you might be taken a bit by surprise as you declare the very nature of yourself that is so often overlooked. It is more usual to discuss or describe anything other than the Self; yet here all at once you are face to face with the Truth about your own Self. It is almost as if a name has been called out, and quite suddenly you realize that the name is your own.

In varying degrees it becomes apparent—"That eternal, free Spirit—*I am That!*" With this great insight, thoughts tend to slow and center inward. Emerging and surpassing other impressions, a deep peace begins to fill the mind as the Truth of the words becomes clearer—*I am eternal, free Spirit!*

H. Emilie Cady called the "I" of each individual "a standing forth of God into visibility." You can perceive that "I" of you standing forth now, strong, loving, peaceful, radiant. It becomes more and more evident that all things really relate to that "I" of you. The passing objects and events in the outer that appear so various and disassociated are pivoted and grounded in That, and That alone. Here is the source of divine certainty, the eternal basis of choice you have been seeking. According to the eternal, free Spirit that is your real nature, choose what you will hold to in life and what you will put aside from you; what must diminish and what must increase; what shall be found out as unreal and what shall be known as real.

Whatever circumstances surround you now, and whatever you may yet meet in life, you will not be swayed! You are divinely helped, balanced, strengthened, and protected from within at all times. You will find the answers you seek, you will overcome the challenges and the seeming setbacks; you will come out of it all victorious.

Give thanks that the strength you need and the fulfillment you seek are within you. Be encouraged! Feel happy and strong, for all things are open to you, eternal, free Spirit!

PATTERN ONE

Learning to Let Go

Lesson 3: Finding the Centers

You have made great discoveries if you have applied yourself to your practice. You have begun to realize that the limits to creative imagination are *imaginary*. There is no idea, however deep or complex, that your mind cannot reach, grasp, develop, and *pass on.* You can accomplish the greatest task your imagination can encompass; you can be the finest, freest person you can envision. You are finding out that, in reality, you are in step with eternity, in tune with the Infinite.

Now no negative concept of time can limit you, no apparent conflict or chaos can keep you from that which you seek. You have already discovered a great treasure in the realm of ideas that can never be lost or taken from you.

You are now realizing the limitless possibilities of your mind. You can already guess that you are not really bound by a limited conception of space. You have stretched your mind beyond time to the idea of eternity; you have reached with your mind to a realization of rhythm and harmony that pervades appearances. In this sense, you have become a "space traveler." Your vehicle is lightning fast, infinitely versatile *thought.* Your constant power source is that "something" within you—that indestructible, undefeatable *Self.*

Within you is the center of the universe. You may climb to the peaks of the earth or descend to cavernous depths, but the center you take with you always. Man has always believed that he must move in relation to the world, but in Truth he discovers that his world moves in relation to him.

> ... at the very center of our being there is something that, in our highest moments, knows itself more than conqueror over all things; it always says, "I can, and I will" *(H. Emilie Cady, How I Used Truth).*

Let go of the false belief that you are controlled by outer conditions of occupation, level of education, financial status, attitudes of family or friends, age, appearance, or present state of health.

These outer conditions that you have patterned your life around can now be placed in proper perspective. You need no longer be constantly buffeted about by conflicting demands of people and circumstances. You are now *mightier* than circumstance through the power within you. You are centered within in perfect strength, perfect peace.

Let these pages drop to your lap for a moment. Close your eyes and think of that center within you as you repeat this statement several times:

I am centered within in perfect strength, perfect peace.

Although you find great peace in contemplating the center within you, you may find that almost instantly your mind begins to wander. Thoughts of surroundings, home, family, work, problems, at once begin to draw you away from your purpose.

This is the time to exercise your power of will. Remind yourself of the goal you set out to find. You made the decision to experience something beyond the ordinary; you resolved to find God. Reestablish yourself in this decision. Use your force of will to direct your mind back to that "something" within you that is eternal, free Spirit, in harmony with the universe, one with God. There is no book or teacher that can take the place of your own firm decision to seek the Truth. Once you have decided, let nothing dissuade you.

If noises in your environment begin to disturb you, direct your mind away from them. Command your thoughts to be centered within. If your body seems to rebel in discomfort when you wish it to remain still, remember that *you* are the master of your senses. Firmly say to yourself:

Peace, be still.

It may be helpful to repeat this affirmation to yourself each time a physical or mental interruption threatens your concentration. Each time some problem or concern comes to your mind, force your mind to release it by saying to your thoughts:

Peace, be still.

Immediately redirect your thoughts to that center of peace within you. Know that here is the source of all strength, all tranquillity.

When this idea becomes more and more real to you, you will derive greater understanding from the following passage:

You realize that you are something like a strong tower against which the winds or waves cannot prevail. You are stabilized.

Even as a high tower has its footing deep in earth so do you have your foundation established deep in Spirit and you are unmoved by capricious winds or adverse beliefs *(Frank B. Whitney, Mightier than Circumstance).*

Pause now for a moment and reread the first half of this lesson. This time read it slowly, not only for content, but to get the "feeling" of the message; earnestly look for deeper significance. Whenever you read a phrase or sentence that has special meaning for you, stop reading for a moment. Close your eyes, drop the pages to your lap, and *listen within.* When the words inspire you with a new idea, or when you begin to *feel* the Truth of a statement, hold the feeling in your mind; register it there so that you can recall it and use it again. Make note of your thoughts and feelings in your Spiritual Diary.

Already you begin to feel that you are "on the brink of something." You begin to thrill to new possibilities, new discoveries. You have begun to let go of all extraneous thoughts and feelings. You are bringing your whole attention to that center within you that is one with God. Everything else revolves around that center; all your actions and affairs are harmonized and blessed through your conscious union with that center of love and strength. When you seek the center of all things, you find it close at hand, immediate—you find it within yourself.

Practice Exercise

Through careful study and thought, your mind is now prepared for a new experience. Sit comfortably, but be attentive to your inner feelings. Read the exercise, then rest your hands in your lap and practice using your imagination as the exercise directs.

Imagine that you are like a strong tower. You are completely stabilized and immovable. No wind can sway you in the slightest. Your foundation is firmly established deep within yourself; you are filled with strength and purpose. You are centered in God in the midst of you.

Be still. Be still. Be still. God in the midst of you is substance. God in the midst of you is love. God in the midst of you is wisdom. Let not your thoughts be

given over to lack, but let wisdom fill
them with the substance and faith of
God. Let not your heart be a center of

resentment and fear and doubt. Be still and know that at this moment it is the altar of God, of love *(Myrtle Fillmore's Healing Letters).*

Direct all your thoughts to that center within. As you are stabilized by this wonderful idea, imagine that a great wind is filling the room. With your eyes closed, you can almost hear and feel this wind, rushing and blowing all around you.

But you remain as still as if you were at the eye of a hurricane. Nothing can disturb or move you. You are steadfast, centered in God in the midst of you. Affirm aloud:

I am steadfast, centered in God in the midst of me. Peace, be still.

You are in tune with the source of all power, all strength. As you acknowledge this power within you by repeating the affirmations above, the wind is at once stilled; calm and a hushed silence pervade the air.

At this time you will feel the peace that has been established within you spreading to fill the entire room. As you get up from your practice, you take this peace with you. You are now steadfast, centered in God in the midst of you.

Whenever thoughts of fear or doubt threaten your peace of mind, remember at once the center of strength and peace that is ever-present within you. Nothing can shake this inner strength, nothing can intrude on the peace you have found.

During the week, it may be helpful to you to review the entire lesson. Add to the material with your own insight as you record the ideas and significant experiences you have in your Spiritual Diary. Take time to consider these questions for yourself:

1. What ideas of Truth about myself, about God, do the lesson and the practice exercise suggest to me?

2. What words, phrases, images, or symbols particularly help me to peacefully center my mind and serve to uplift my thoughts and feelings beyond worry and distraction? (Here I begin lists or diagrams of these special aids.)

3. Have there been times in my life when I have knowingly or unknowingly "centered inward" to reach an awareness of strength and calm? What was the result?

4. Are there any potentially disturbing or fearful conditions in my life now that I

might meet more victoriously by consciously focusing on my own indwelling
center of power and peace?

5. In what ways am I now unfolding?

When you look at these notes and build on
them in days to come, you will be reminded
of the source of peace you had discovered.

Pattern One

Lesson 4

Dear Student:

Inwardly give thanks as you share this great realization with the Psalmist:

> "The Lord is my light and my salvation;
>   whom shall I fear?
> The Lord is the stronghold of my life;
>   of whom shall I be afraid?

> One thing have I asked of the Lord,
>   that will I seek after;
> That I may dwell in the house of the Lord
>   all the days of my life,
> to behold the beauty of the Lord,
>   and to inquire in his temple"
>   *(Psalms 27:1, 4).*

As you think of these words, you feel enfolded and fortified by divine love, and the mind begins to dwell in thoughts of light and peace. Often in these lessons it is suggested that you allow the mind to dwell on an idea. When the mind rests in an idea of Truth, a sensation of inner light or illumination is present in varying degrees of intensity. You begin to become peacefully and powerfully "single-minded," in the way that a ray of sunlight focused through a magnifying glass is concentrated. Great penetrating and purifying power is the result—power to literally burn up hindering, confusing, or depressing thought habits and to light up all aspects of life and understanding.

This peace, this inner light, is soon placed above all else for while it is the experience in life that seems most rare and precious, yet it is free to all and available at every turn. The student of Truth reaches the point in his unfoldment when as he contemplates the idea of absolute peace and blessedness, it is as if he inwardly resolves: "Nothing else but this will do! I must experience this! 'One thing have I asked of the Lord, that will I seek after.' " And as you reach this point you, too, find that the longing to attain and prolong this unique awareness grows and grows.

Leaving apathy behind and breaking free of the mental inertia that is so difficult to overcome, you are moved by a new force of inertia—that of irresistible movement toward the spiritual ideal. In this way you are ever urged and speeded onward.

It is true that in this spiritual search the senses may seem to become more delicate, apparently more acutely aware than ever before of the sweetness and goodness of life; yet you realize at the same time that you must experience directly that which sweetens all of life . . . that by whose light even the brightest sun in the universe shines; that which is self-luminous within as the eternal light of divine consciousness.

You may perceive that this inner light, while ever constant, is neither cold, unresponsive, nor inactive by any means, but is dynamic living power! Herein lies understanding and illumination; here is the overcoming, all-withstanding strength you need to do everything that needs to be done by you.

You have touched the Source of all strength and power, you are consciously centered in absolute peace. Now joyfully welcome the dawn of spiritual light that reveals all things to you. Allow the mind to dwell on the idea of great spiritual light as you begin this lesson. Know that your future is bright with infinite blessings!

PATTERN ONE

Learning to Let Go

Lesson 4: Opening to the Light

By this time surely you are experiencing a particular sensation of blessedness each day when you return to your chosen study place. Through your own sincere efforts, you have built in this time and place an atmosphere of peace and inspiration that in turn fortifies and sanctifies you.

Now you can scarcely pass by this chair or think of it during the day without the thought of spiritual experience coming to your mind. Every time you return to this place, your mind tends to follow its natural inclination toward the Truth. When you finish your lesson, you feel refreshed and renewed. This place has now become a good and useful

61

"laboratory"—it is cleansed and ordered for spiritual discovery. You have set up a good culture for constructive ideas, a climate to receive insight.

In this atmosphere of mental expectancy, no truth is too great but that your thought can expand to include it. You are in the process of mental "stretching." You are learning to let go of false beliefs of limitation; you are learning freedom. You are learning that through rightly controlling your mind, you can actually *experience Truth.*

You have found that experiencing Truth is like meeting again a friend you have not seen for a long time. You have forgotten the place where you knew him, and the name you knew him by, but something about him is familiar, unforgettable. At first, you feel only a vague attraction. But suddenly he speaks to you, your hands touch, and all at once you *recognize* him.

So it is when you discover a truth. At first you simply feel agreeable toward the idea; you have the feeling that something within you *corresponds* to it in some way. As you open your mind to it, as you reach out for it, suddenly you experience the Truth. Instantly *recognition* occurs; you accept the idea as reality. Darkness and uncertainty vanish in the light of this realization.

Last week you experienced a truth about yourself by focusing all your attention within you. Right now, turn back to the Practice Exercise in the preceding chapter. As you read it once again, let your mind follow its suggestions. Pause when you have finished reading it; hold the experience in your mind.

As you remain attentive to this center of peace within you, you may have the sensation of warmth or light. When you close your eyes for a moment and think of it, you can almost "see" this inner source of light; you can begin to feel secure, enfolded, illumined.

Now you can guess why throughout the history of mankind, light and warmth have been associated with divinity. It is true that light and warmth have been essential to man's physical existence, but it is also true that somehow the experience of light and warmth is characteristic of the spiritual feeling of closeness to God.

You have discovered within you a center of light and warmth, an unfailing source of peace and love. God within you is eternal, changeless, perfect wisdom and harmony. When you acknowledge this truth about yourself, your entire life undergoes a wonderful transformation.

You will feel differently about yourself when the light of your spiritual nature sheds its radiance upon every part of your life.

When the light of understanding dawns upon us, it warms us, and love is quickened within us. We commence to respond to the spiritual urge within us to express more and more of the goodness of God *(May Rowland, Dare to Believe!).*

Expand your thinking to include these inspiring ideas. As you study this quotation, mentally "stretch" to reach its meaning.

As you think about "light" and "radiance," you will find it difficult to dwell at the same time on thoughts of sickness, bitterness, or limitation of any kind. Light cannot really be contained or confined, but is perfectly free. It seems to be essentially purifying, beautifying, life-giving. It is naturally incompatible with darkness; the two cannot exist together.

When you accept the idea that a source of perfect light is ever shining within you, you cannot think of yourself as ill or poor. Within you is the source of infinite strength and health; within you is a radiant treasure beyond words. Bitterness and foolishness fade like shadows when you are focused on this great light. You realize that God within you is infinite love, infinite wisdom. He is manifest in you as the light of your spiritual nature.

Pause here for a moment. Put down your papers and consciously center your attention on the source of light within you. As you think of all the good attributes of warmth and light, "listen" and "watch" within and remember what you feel.

You will notice a definite feeling of love when you are completely attentive to the idea of the center of perfect light within you. Make note of this feeling in your Spiritual Diary. As you prepare to develop this experience in the following Practice Exercise, affirm:

God within me radiates perfect love.

Begin now to open your mind and heart to this feeling. Repeat the statement once again as you make ready to experience this Truth.

Practice Exercise

As you think of God's perfect love radiating within you, shining through every part of your being, consider the following passage:

A consciousness of light, an awareness of spiritual illumination, is the first step in the healing of any personal difficulty, even as it was the first step in the process of creation. 'And God said, Let there be light: and there was light.'. . . The true spiritual light, our first step in understanding and overcoming, is worth awaiting in our silent periods of prayer, worth our time and patience and application of faith, even as the dawn is worthy of all nature's quiet attention. The awakening of our souls anew to eternal spiritual truths and values cannot come any other way *(Mary Kupferle, God Never Fails).*

Sit comfortably, but maintain an attentive physical as well as mental posture. Suggest an attitude of expectancy to your mind by affirming:

I am guided by the light of God within me, I am open and receptive to His love.

Read through the exercise, letting your mind get the "feeling" of the words. Then close your eyes and use your imagination to gain the experience of this Truth.

Imagine that you are sitting alone on a vast plain. The sunrise has not yet come, and all is in darkness. As you sit waiting, you are completely still. There is no sound or movement to disturb you.

All at once you perceive the first rays of the sun on the horizon. Slowly, more and more sunlight is visible, until at last it shines in full glory before you.

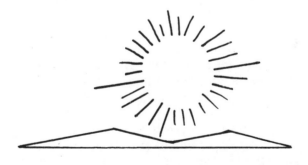

As you bask in the warm, healing, strengthening light, you are filled with a feeling of infinite love. Sunshine fills the air all around you—there is light everywhere.

Think of this light as God's love, surrounding and enfolding you. As you breathe easily and rhythmically, you feel you are actually inhaling this wonderful sunlight. Open your lungs, your every cell to receive this light as you open your mind and heart to receive God's infinite love.

The radiance of this love surrounds you, enfolds you, and shines through every part of your body. Perfect healing and light pervade your being. All the "dark corners" of your thinking and affairs are filled with perfect purifying light.

Now hold the feeling. When beliefs of sickness, resentment, or lack begin to intrude on your thinking, close your eyes for a moment and feel the sunshine of this idea:

The radiance of God's love shines in me and through me.

Each time you recall this experience, you will feel quickened and awakened to new life and vitality. The experience at once prompts you to be active, creative, constantly growing and becoming a more perfect expression of

God's love.

If you look into a mirror right now, you will actually see a new radiance shining in your face. Everyone you meet will be blessed by your bright smile and loving way as you continue to express God's love. Each time you see your reflection in a mirror, silently affirm:

The radiance of God's love shines in you and through you.

You have made a great discovery. You have experienced something wonderful! As you keep your Spiritual Diary, consider the effects on your thinking of the idea of inner light. Ask yourself, "In what ways am I now unfolding?" Write down in your notes the many good things that happen to you as you practice this exercise daily and as you learn to feel and express God's love—the love that is ever-present, ever-shining within you.

Through the next pattern of lessons and exercises, you will be guided to a fuller, deeper understanding of your world.

Pattern Two
Lesson 1

Dear Student:

As you prepare to begin Pattern Two, give thanks for the great things that have happened to you already. As you look back through your notes, you find that you have made great progress. Yet somehow in gaining understanding through these first steps, you have an even greater longing to *learn* more, to *do* more.

Each time you sat down to study, you probably found the exercises to be easier, more natural for you, until at last you began to gain a new experience that was suggestive of many more wonderful experiences to come.

It may be that although you have felt very

inspired at the very beginning of a practice, the struggle to control the mind seemed increasingly difficult for a few days thereafter. You must never allow such "setbacks" to discourage you, for your great desire and the unfailing inner wisdom and strength will carry you through. Although the search demands courage and perseverance, the treasure you seek is wonderful beyond words, and you will find it!

PATTERN TWO

Learning to Reach Out

Lesson 1: Seeing Beauty

Last week you began to learn to "let go" of imaginary limits and negative thoughts, and to grasp a new meaning to your life. You have discovered a source of strength within you that can carry you through any difficulty, lift you over any obstacle. A new feeling has been awakened, a new longing to keep these wonderful ideas in your mind every moment, to remain absorbed in this experience of inner peace throughout each day.

But already you know that this undertaking is far more difficult than it may seem. Although your mind has an inclination toward the truth you have experienced, it may be that as soon as you open your eyes after your exercise, the beautiful feeling you have gained seems to deteriorate before the scenes and experiences of the "everyday."

You have touched that part of you that is eternal, perfect harmony, perfect peace, self-luminous love. How magnificent is this experience! And yet somehow the radiance of this feeling does seem to fade somewhat as you continue to live and work in a world that seems to you to be so imperfect. As your thinking turns to the faults of people and circumstances, it becomes increasingly difficult to feel peaceful and happy.

You know that if the experiences of inner peace you have had are to help you, if they are really to change your life, they must be verified, carried into every phase of your life. It must be possible for you to relate your inner feelings to everyone and everything around you. You have established a base of experience—a beginning. Now you will begin to reach out from that base to new discoveries and new application of Truth.

If you believe that you live in a world of ugliness, distortion, and chaos, then for you, the world will be a terrible place. But if you choose instead to look for beauty and order in the world, then you will *find* beauty and order. You will see the finest works of art all around you every moment. It is not necessary to go to an art gallery to find beauty; it is only necessary to bring your vision into focus—to look more carefully and lovingly at your environment.

The world can be yours to mold according to a higher pattern when, instead of agreeing with error, or fighting it, you bring into your world your highest ideals and ideas and look straight through its pretensions to the design for a better life that has been shown you within *(Winifred Wilkinson, Focus on Living)*.

Think of it—"the world can be *yours to mold.*" In your own unique and inspired way, you endlessly *create* your world. By your attitude, by your own idea of what life is like, you constantly choose the pattern in which you see yourself.

All things that are formed originated with an idea. Every building, machine, lamp, dinner plate, or pencil is formed according to someone's *idea*. Consider that the universe, in all its myriad forms and aspects, is created in accordance with *God's idea.* Realizing that there is a "higher pattern" behind all things, you consciously seek the underlying goodness and beauty in the world. In this way you become attuned to God's divine idea; you get "in touch" with God.

At the end of this sentence, pause for a moment and visualize a beautiful sunset you have seen, or a wheat field blowing in the wind, or a delicate rose.

There is something special about that experience, something that takes you out of the ordinary. When you see beauty in the world, you feel suddenly lighter, happier, wiser than usual. You feel that you are perceiving something that is true, that *corresponds to something within you.* For a second or a minute, you look into the very heart of things. Here is a meaning to life that cannot be written down.

We do not need speculation to prove that life has meaning, any more than we need a discourse on the laws of light to

74

prove that a rainbow or a sunset has meaning *(James Dillet Freeman, Be!)*.

Remember that some of the exercises you practiced in Pattern One were related to beauty in nature. These exercises were chosen because it seems easy and natural for people to forget about imperfections and troubles in life and to feel a breathless awe when confronted with nature's splendor. When you look at something that you think is truly beautiful, you are lifted to a feeling of peace and worship.

You begin to perceive that the Creator of the universe could not be a silent, stony God. You begin to know that He is an eternally expressive, infinitely artistic God.

It seems that man has always had this natural inclination to appreciate beauty in the world, to find in nature the seed of heroism, of divinity. Men in all places and times have looked at brilliant sunsets, fascinating waters, intricate leaves, and have felt that same stirring that you also feel when you see something beautiful. Out of this common enthusiasm for beauty in nature, people have constantly expressed hints of nature's color and design in their art and decoration.

You may begin to understand why man's places of worship are often decorated with beautiful pictures, stained-glass windows, and many other fine ornaments. One reason for this is that the experience of beauty somehow *transports* human thinking to a state of wonder, of peace.

Worship comes naturally to man when he is surrounded with beautiful things. He forgets himself. He becomes absorbed in beauty. Man experiences a communion with the creation. He begins to see God in the world.

Through this common experience comes the understanding "that there is nothing that is·not unique, special, important, meaningful" *(James Dillet Freeman)*. For those who have developed this experience, the world becomes like a great curiosity shop, filled with wonderful and lovely things.

From the most vivid and perfect rose to the plainest little stone, everything takes on a new significance. Even apparent disorder and ugliness become beautiful to one who can keep in mind that everything is part of a divine pattern—an idea in the mind of God.

When you have practiced and exercised an attitude of love for the world, you learn to look at life like a child on Christmas morning. You forget to find fault with your surroundings, for you begin to see in people and situations the beauty and the good you have overlooked before.

One person may look at a stone and see only a piece of gravel. He kicks it out of his path and hurries on. Another person may take the time to stop and look. Instead of just a piece of gravel, he sees an interesting rock formation, a natural "artwork." The person who hurried on missed the color and design of the rock completely. He also missed an opportunity to see something beautiful. But the person who looked creatively was able to appreciate the beauty of the stone. He takes with him a pleasant sensation, an impression of beauty.

The extra time the creative person took was really only a second or two. But the man in a hurry missed a great opportunity. He missed a chance to know and express the truth that he lives and moves in God's good time. He failed to see meaning and importance in a seemingly plain and insignificant object because he could not see a higher significance in all things.

However, when you consciously look for goodness and beauty, you find it easier to forget personal hurts and fears just as a child forgets a scraped knee when someone hands him a toy. In this way, your world is transformed, remolded through your new attitude. What once may have seemed a dreary world becomes a magical, beautiful world.

You can keep with you an attitude of loving appreciation. The lifted feeling you have when you have just come from an art gallery, someone's lovely home, a quiet garden, or a green forest need not fade when you learn to maintain a creative outlook.

There is no need to fabricate a dream paradise in your imagination. You do not seek a dream world, but a better understanding, a closer communion with the *real* world. You have learned that harmony and peace is established within you, and can be experienced *right now*. Stretch your thinking to realize that *paradise can be experienced right here.*

The idea of paradise is not merely a dream, but a reality. The world you live in, the nation, state, city, street, house, room you occupy right now, is paradise when you learn to really see beauty in life. Stop here for a moment and dwell on this thought before you go on to the exercise:

Right now, I live in paradise.

Practice Exercise

Hold the thought that the world in which you live is *paradise*. At first you may feel your mind struggle against this idea. Surely there seems to be much that should be improved in the conditions of the world. But there is also much that is beautiful and good that has been passed by. When you learn to think and see beyond the apparent lack and distortion in the world, you find that this expansion of thought serves a dual purpose. First, you will experience a temporary but refreshing suspension of preoccupation with whatever may have been troubling you. Then, more and more, you will begin to perceive that life has a background of changeless good. Your outlook begins to change and broaden. You begin to see that life represents a constant opportunity to experience every aspect of paradise.

Right now, decide that you will not miss this great opportunity. Affirm for yourself:

I look lovingly and creatively at the world,

and I see beauty everywhere.

Choose some object in the room that is beautiful to you. It may be a picture on the wall, a lamp, or a piece of jewelry. Look at this object closely, observing carefully its color, form, and the way the light strikes it. Learn to witness what you feel; register in your mind this feeling of appreciation. It is a pleasant experience, an experience that helps you momentarily to lose sight of personal problems. You are transported out of yourself and into a greater awareness.

Now choose something else that is beautiful, something that you may never have noticed before. It may be the pattern of a bedspread, drapery, or rug. It may be the interesting shape of a drawer pull, or the border of a picture frame.

Whatever it may be, search for something that you have never really looked at before. If at first you feel that nothing you haven't noticed before in the room is particularly beautiful, look again; search more carefully. Explore the endless possibilities around you. The grain of wood at the door frame, or the shadow of a chair, may represent great beauty you had never found before. When you have found something new, look at it closely and lovingly. Observe its qualities of beauty and register in your mind what you feel.

Every day when you look for something new to appreciate, you will begin to feel that you could go on forever finding beauty. When you have learned to look more lovingly and creatively at your surroundings, you find that *everything* is beautiful in some way.

As you practice the exercise of looking for beauty each day, remember to expand the exercise to include all your activities. It may not always be easy at first to see beauty in people and situations. But as you consciously look for good around you, you find that life becomes better and more beautiful.

This week consciously bless all things. Practice a loving attitude toward the world. When there seems to be a flaw in something, look for the good in it; praise it silently. Even when someone you meet seems to have a very irritating manner, silently bless this person. To bless is to "invoke good upon; to call forth the action of God; to confer God's good on something or someone" *(Charles Fillmore, The Revealing Word).*

Then when you return to your study place

each day, reread the Practice Exercise to remind yourself of this wonderful activity of
seeking the best in life. List the new discoveries of beauty and goodness you recognize this week in your Spiritual Diary notes.
Then at the end of your practice each day,
close your eyes and visualize all that is beautiful and good that you have found. Consider
the ways in which you are now unfolding.
Give thanks to God that the world is so beautiful, and that life is so good. Remember to
affirm as you close your study time:

*I look lovingly and creatively at the world,
and I see beauty everywhere.*

Pattern Two

Lesson 2

Dear Student:

Always keep encouraged, even though you find that trying to control the mind is like trying to control the wind. Just when it seems you have completely shut out an unwanted habit of thinking, it rushes in again to challenge you. One day you feel as if you are soaring; the next, you are inexplicably "earthbound" again. At times the words on these pages will seem to *speak* to you; you feel the thrill of joyful acknowledgment and you think, "Yes, yes . . . I *know* this is true." Then suddenly the mind may seem to turn traitor; thousands of doubts appear to tempt you away from your goal.

As you unfold, remember that a healthy

skepticism is in your interest as a student of Truth. You need only accept what you can experience for yourself. But be sure that you do not become like a man who is so uncertain and critical about entering a house that he spends the whole day quarreling with himself and pacing back and forth outside the door, never going in at all.

Do not be concerned if you experience doubt and confusion; these are the experiences of all seekers of Truth. At such times of challenge, use your will to banish hindering thoughts. Hold before your mind the goal you have resolved to attain. Let nothing in your life or thought be an obstacle to that decision!

Continue to let go of all negative, hindering thoughts and hold fast to the Truth you have found through the experiences you were led to in previous lessons. Give thanks for the understanding you have gained, and for the challenge of the lessons to come!

PATTERN TWO

Learning to Reach Out

Lesson 2: Accepting Good

In the first Pattern you made the discovery that there is a center within you that radiates peace and love. Now as you learn to look for beauty and goodness in the world around you, you feel the love radiating from within you, shining forth into every aspect of your world to bring forth its beauty and order.

As you learn to look for beauty around you, the feeling of appreciation increases, and your world becomes a paradise. You now know how to look creatively at life, and at other people. You have begun to practice the art of appreciation.

Every art requires distinctive training and steadfast practice, and that of appreciation is no exception. . . .

He who would be versed in this finest of fine arts must learn its technique and live and work accordingly. He must have "the hearing ear, and the seeing eye,". . . the desire to praise whatever is worthy both in others and in himself. As

he understands life from this viewpoint,
he cannot fail to recognize its privileges
and its possibilities *(Richard J. Lynch,
The Unity Treasure Chest).*

You are developing a receptive attitude to
things around you; you are mentally opening
up to life, and reaching out with your mind
for the good that is everywhere waiting for
you. As you mentally praise your surroundings, you begin to recognize their beauty and
their great possibilities.

When you look for beauty and good, you
are not necessarily seeking to possess everything you see. Your mind is not fixed on
monetary value or on contemporary fashion.
Rather, you are looking for a timeless quality
of beauty that is not relative to material
worth. This quality of eternal beauty that is
discoverable in all things suggests the great
possibility that the universe is *absolutely* good
and beautiful.

This realization is well worth the "steadfast
practice" that the art of true appreciation requires. A kind of mental stretch is involved—a
"reaching" activity in your thinking helps you
to appreciate and touch the good in life.

When you are deeply moved by a poignant

speech or poem, by someone's dramatic or sentimental gesture, or by the sight of a golden sunset or a lovely rose garden, you may say that you are "touched." It is not that anyone or anything has come into direct physical contact with you, but that somehow you have reached an intangible contact. Perhaps you find within yourself a point of correspondence to all that is beautiful and good. You respond to beauty subjectively. You are sympathetic, you "feel with" the beauty of the idea or the sight.

But in order to appreciate something beautiful or "touching," you must first *listen* to the dramatic speaker, *read* the moving words, or *look* at the beautiful rose. If you sleep through the opera, you will miss the experience completely. If the book remains on the table unopened, you cannot read and be affected by the message it contains. If you walk by the rose garden without looking down, you will not see the beauty there.

You must open your eyes and look for beauty. You must watch for it, listen for it, reach for it with your senses and with your mind. Although there is beauty everywhere, you must make the effort to see it, to experience it. You must make the effort to expand your capacity to appreciate it.

You begin to realize that the true business of life is developing a *capacity* to live. You seek a fuller capacity to feel more peaceful, to live more harmoniously, more lovingly, and to experience more of the inherent goodness and beauty of life. But just as you must exercise your body to develop a physical muscle, you need to exercise your mental and emotional "muscles" to receive more of life's goodness. You must stretch your thinking and feeling capacity.

Michelangelo's familiar painting of the hand of God reaching to touch the hand of man inspires a greater understanding of this thought. God reaches out to you in every single moment, from every atom of the creation, extending to you infinite Truth, infinite beauty, infinite goodness. The strength each person must develop seems paltry compared to the strength of God, but this individual effort is necessary nevertheless. Man's small reaching out is necessary to complete the avenue so that God can rush in.

You know from your experiences that through even a small effort to see goodness and beauty around you, the pleasure you receive far exceeds the effort you expend. You find it seems to be the nature of the world, the nature of God, to *respond* to you as soon as you become really receptive, as soon as you begin to seek Truth actively and sincerely. As you develop an open and loving attitude to the world, you immediately feel a loving response. You gain the feeling of being surrounded and enfolded with goodness.

Perhaps you feel so much "at home" in your own home because you have chosen and arranged your own possessions and furnishings, because you can see potential comfort and beauty in them. You see the *good* in them, so that when you are among these things, you feel comfortable and secure. You feel that you are "at home."

When you learn to see the good possibilities in all things, you develop a sense of being "at home" in all places and under all conditions. You can look at life lovingly and creatively, seeing the good even in apparently bad situations.

When you have achieved this attitude toward life, you will retain your individual preferences for certain colors and styles. You will still find it easier to see beauty in some things than in others, but you will have found an underlying goodness in life.

In the same way that an artist steps back from his subject to get an idea of composition, to see it in its entirety, you can take a "step back" from appearances in life to get a clearer look. You see that just as a painting has a background, life also has a background—a background of perfection. You can then know for yourself:

I look upon a world of beauty. I am lifted to a consciousness* of noble and beautiful things. I see my world filled with that which is beautiful and blessed. I see the people and the things of my world expressing and manifesting the beauty of God back of all life *(Frank B. Whitney)*.

---

*consciousness—The sense of awareness, of knowing. The knowledge or realization of any idea, object, or condition. The sum total of all ideas accumulated in and affecting man's present being. . . .

It is very important to understand the importance of our consciousness in spiritual growth. Divine ideas must be incorporated into our consciousness before they can mean anything to us. An intellectual concept does not suffice (Charles Fillmore, The Revealing Word).

In developing an increased capacity for Truth, you are "lifted to a consciousness of noble and beautiful things." To enter into this consciousness, you must let go of an imperfect conception of yourself and of the world. You mentally "stretch" to reach and touch the truth about life. When you feel a point of contact with God—when you feel you are "touching" the Infinite, and when you feel "touched" by God, true prayer begins.

From your experiences in Lesson 1 of this Pattern, you know that the world is naturally beautiful, that this beauty suggests to you an ideal pattern, an underlying goodness in the universe. The natural result of this idea is a feeling of appreciation, of love for the world, of joyful acceptance of all that life holds.

But you also know that you must actively prepare yourself to seek and receive inspiration in life. You must reach out with your mind and heart for the good that awaits you. With these ideas in mind, proceed to your practice exercise.

Practice Exercise

Mentally review the good things you see during the day. Visualize a graceful tree, the magnificent sky, a smiling face, a loving look, all that is good and beautiful that comes into your life. You are building an attitude of loving acceptance of God's bountiful good. Acknowledge this acceptance by affirming:

I behold the good in life, I receive it joyously.

You have read that to feel touched by life's beauty, to feel moved by it, revitalized by it, you must actively seek and accept this good. God, the good omnipotent,* extends to you infinite blessings at this moment and every moment. You have but to open your mind, stretch your thinking, reach out to receive this wonderful truth.

*omnipotence—Infinite power. God is infinite power. All the power there is. All-powerful (Charles Fillmore, The Revealing Word).

Read the rest of the practice exercise, then put aside your lesson. Try to practice thinking and feeling as the exercise suggests. Although some amount of self-discipline may be needed at first, try to hold the mental and physical attitude of receptivity for several minutes. Although time should never be a depressing restriction on your activities, it can serve as an aid in practicing self-control and spiritual development.

As you begin to direct your thoughts in a peaceful, constructive way, affirm this statement:

I behold the good in life, I receive it joyously.

As you hold to this wonderful idea, sit with spine erect, both feet on the floor. Extend your arms forward so that your hands rest, palms upward, on your knees. As you close your eyes, feel that your mind is completely receptive to all that is good, all that is beautiful.

Know that just as your hands are open, so also your mind and heart are open and ready to receive God's infinite blessings. Speak these positive words:

I lovingly reach out with my mind and heart, and I receive God's abundant good.

If your mind begins to wander from your purpose, repeat the affirmations given above to redirect your thoughts. Whenever an idea comes to your mind of something particularly beautiful, the thought of someone you know, a lovely sight you have seen, or some inspiring words, acknowledge all good as the gift of

God, and receive it joyously.

Know that as you maintain this loving, receptive attitude, all experiences and persons that come into your life are seen in a wonderful new light. Not only do you *perceive* the good that is in people and situations, but your open, loving attitude has a way of *bringing out* this good. As you express a joyous acceptance of life, you discover that those you meet begin to respond to you in an increasingly loving and helpful way. New avenues of activity begin to open up to you. Creative ideas and new insights begin to come to you more and more easily. Be sure to make note of your experiences this week as your mind becomes open and receptive to the infinite potential of life. This loving direction of your thoughts will bring wonderful results in your life!

Ideas for consideration in your Spiritual Diary:

What particular sights have you seen this week that have particularly impressed you? Describe them and the feeling you had when you experienced them.

Make note of the favorite poems, quotations, or ideas that particularly "touch" you. What kind of mood or feeling do these ideas create in you?

You have read that God is omnipotent; how would you rephrase this concept?

How does the concept that God is omnipotent affect your understanding of your own relationship to God?

In what ways are you now unfolding?

Pattern Two
Lesson 3

Dear Student:

The Truth is here for you to know for yourself! It is all around you just as the air is all around you. Others have sought and found it already. It may be that many other students began this course on the very same day that you began it. They read these words with you today; they struggle with you, pray with you, experience with you, and rejoice with you.

Let neither discouragement nor haughtiness enter your thinking. The search for Truth is the pursuit of all mankind, consciously or unconsciously. Others have searched as you do, search with you now, and will search in the future. There is nothing that you have learned that has not been learned by others;

yet there is nothing that others have realized and demonstrated that you may not also realize and demonstrate!

Truth is really the discovery of people in all ages and nations. It pervades the world like the air; you need only watch for it, listen for it, think of it. In doing this, you touch a certainty about life, a source of peace, harmony, security, *Truth*. In exercising your creative imagination, you have touched Truth, and *it has touched you*. It is the very center of you, the very life of your life. Hold to it, live by it. As you accept this challenge, realize that you are united with students of Truth throughout the world by the experience you share. As you think of all other students, affirm for each other:

We are guided by divine wisdom, united and blessed by God's infinite love.

As you hold other students in loving thoughts of praise, *you* are strengthened and blessed by the love and praise of thousands. Truly, God is in the midst of you right now!

PATTERN TWO

Learning to Reach Out

Lesson 3: Divine Connection

In Pattern One, Lesson 3, you practiced turning your thoughts to the center within you of peace and strength. That center is changeless, self-luminous, constantly close at hand. After the initial struggle with interfering thoughts and restless senses, you become still and concentrate on the source of strength within yourself. Soon you experience a flood of peace, an intense feeling of well-being. You know that you are capable of great things. As this feeling of inner goodness grows, you actually *radiate* peace and love. It is now natural to look for good in all things, to seek and experience more and more beauty in all aspects of existence.

At this point you become aware of an inherent goodness and perfection in the "background" of life. Something in and behind the world of appearances is as changeless and perfect as that center of peace and strength within yourself.

"There is an inmost center in us and

in the world, an inmost center where there is order and peace and a dynamic potentiality for good. When we know this, we know life as a whole, and not simply as a partial experience" *(Eric Butterworth, Unity of All Life).*

Consider how all things are unified through this "dynamic potentiality for good." When you are conscious of this underlying goodness, this all-pervading unity in the universe, you learn to take a step back from a limited "close-up" view of life and, like an artist stepping back to survey his canvas, you get a fuller, more balanced concept of the whole. What seemed to be mere blotches and lines at close range begin to show order and direction, meaning and purpose.

When you are truly receptive to goodness and beauty, you cease to see life as a series of fragmented, disassociated experiences. For example, if you were to lift a letter of the alphabet out of the context of this printed page, it would appear to be an isolated, unrelated, and therefore insignificant symbol. But taken in the context of the page as a whole, each letter contributes to the total meaning of a word; words in turn make up sentences, which take on an even greater meaning in paragraphs, and so complete, related thoughts are expressed.

If you examine with a microscope a print of a photograph in a book or magazine, you see thousands of tiny dots without apparent significance. But when you see the whole at once, the relationship between the thousands of dots of various colors and shading becomes obvious.

Somehow in the intricate relationship between these many small elements, a beautiful picture is formed. A complete pattern emerges with delicate design, striking contrast, finely balanced composition. Each dot contributes to the whole; each is vital to the picture, for each expresses a part of the beauty of the total design. But just as in life, in order to see the complete and beautiful whole, you must reach beyond appearances.

"Appearances are deceptive, but they are not meant to delude or befool or betray us. They are meant for us to study and translate and transmute . . . apparent evil is often actual good.

"No, God did not set out to deceive us. But He meant that we should not

101

fool ourselves. He meant us to use the endowment He gave us to search out truth. He did not conceal truth from us; He illustrated it in a million ways; and one of the ways was to show us that appearances are not always immediate, obvious representations of truth. He gave us the senses to perceive that the spring appears to bubble out of the ground without a source, but He gave us the reason that argues that it must come from somewhere and the ability to understand ultimately that the rain and melting snows on the mountain peak furnish the water that seeps down through the slopes and finally comes up in the seemingly sourceless spring.

"Appearances are relative. They are not the truth, but they are related to truth. They are guides to truth if we only dig into them deeply enough. They lead us to dig, if we do not merely take them at their face value and assume that they have nothing back of them, that they are the facts of life" *(Gardner Hunting, Prove Me Now).*

In looking for the truth that lies "back of"

appearances, in seeking out the real "facts of life," it is often necessary to take a step backward—a step back from a limited perception of the world, a step backward out of the drama of life. You need to take a step into yourself, back to your base of inner light, inner understanding.

As you reach out for Truth, you begin to see that practical religion is often an abnegating process, a process of denying* false appearances in life and affirming that which is true according to a higher understanding.

*"By denial we mean declaring not to be true a thing that seems true. Negative appearances are directly opposed to the teachings of Truth. Jesus said, 'Do not judge by appearances, but judge with right judgment'" (H. Emilie Cady, Lessons in Truth).

This activity is much like peeling an artichoke to get to the sweet heart. In the same way, to make real spiritual progress, you must peel away false notions about the world and about yourself. You must begin to identify yourself not with negative appearances, but with the pure Source of all good. Life is a "seemingly sourceless spring" only until you trace backward to its ultimate Source—God, the good omnipotent.

"There is but one Source of being. This Source is the living fountain of all good, be it life, love, wisdom, power— the Giver of all good gifts. This Source and you are connected, every moment of your existence" *(H. Emilie Cady, Lessons in Truth).*

As you read over this passage, consider carefully its meaning. Repeat aloud the words:

There is but one Source of being. This Source is the living fountain of all good, be it life, love, wisdom, power—the Giver of all good gifts.

Now pause for a moment. Allow these great ideas to really penetrate your mind.

Remember that "this Source and you are connected, every moment of your existence." Right now, at this very moment, you are connected to this Source of all good. When you acknowledge this truth, you know that there can be no lack, no loneliness in your life.

When you realize that *you* are a vital part of God's pattern, eternally connected to the

Infinite, you know that perfect harmony, perfect peace, perfect beauty belong to you. You are in immediate, loving relationship to God. You have found a point of contact, an unbreakable connection with the fountain of all good.

The wonderful truth about this connection is that just as you receive bountifully when your mind and heart are open and receptive to God, so also His blessings are expressed through you. His love, His peace, His strength shine forth in your life to manifest wholeness in every phase of your life and affairs.

Life becomes a complete, circular connection of love and blessings as God's good flows *to* you and *through* you when you express and share the good you receive. The biological interdependence of life is often diagrammed as a continuous, circular activity, representing an ideal balance, a perfect, complete cycle wherein nothing is wasted or lost, but all matter and all forms of life are continually part of the whole pattern of life.

In the same way, life is seen as a whole when you step back from apparent separation and contradiction and consciously acknowledge your connection with God. With this

105

awareness of divine connection between yourself and all things comes a tremendous sense of satisfaction. It is not that larger house or new car or beautiful wardrobe that will make your life complete after all. It is that larger outlook, that new idea, that beautiful way of living.

The chair you sit in at this moment touches the floor, which touches the walls, which touch the foundation, which touches the earth, which touches all things on this planet, which is surrounded by the atmosphere, which touches all space; so on into infinity the divine connection continues. You are part of this connection, through which you touch all things, all people. You and the universe exist in God in the never-ending cycle of life. You are divinely connected to all life, all good. In reality, there can be no separation, no isolation in the universe.

As in a circle diagram of ideal balance in nature, your connection with God in and through all things is an eternal, complete, circular relationship. Think of this divine connection not as "one way," but as a dynamic, vibrant, constant interchange of love, and prepare yourself to *experience* this reality.

Practice Exercise

Step 1. Calm your mind. Consciously disconnect your thoughts from anything that has been a source of worry or regret to you. "Switch off" anxieties as you mentally connect yourself to thoughts of peace and wholeness. Declare aloud:

I disconnect my mind from negative thoughts and feelings, for I am now completely open and receptive to God's good.

As you enter into this calmness, if your mind should tend toward any unwanted thought or feeling, reaffirm the statement above. At first, the sentence may seem too long to remember. But if you patiently consider its meaning as you repeat the words, you will find that the affirmation becomes increasingly effective and at the same time easier to remember. Use the first line of the statement as a denial, an aid to "peel away" false, unwanted thoughts. The second line can be used to help you channel your thinking in a positive, constructive way so that the exercise will be especially meaningful for you.

Step 2. As always, sit in your study place with spine straight, but not stiff. Place both feet on the floor. Again, place your hands, palms upward, on your knees. This physical attitude should aid you in achieving a mental attitude of calm receptivity.

Step 3. Imagine that you are part of a perfect circle. Breathe easily and evenly as you imagine that the air you breathe flows to you and through you and to you again to form a perfect circle of constant flow.

As you breathe in, you feel a lifted sensation when the air fills your lungs. Without halting or breaking the "circle," breathe out again, imagining that in this way the circle is complete. Inhale and exhale with a continuous, even rhythm. Breathe neither too rapidly nor too slowly, but in a natural, even way.

Step 4. When you have established a rhythm to your breathing, and when the idea of an in-and-out flow seems comfortable to you, begin to feel that you are actually inhaling God's good, and that as you exhale, you are giving forth into your life and the lives of those around you the expression of God's love, God's infinite blessings.

Although at first this exercise may be a little challenging for you, if you discipline yourself to daily practice, you will find that each day you will gain a new and satisfying experience of wholeness and unity in life. Record your personal progress in your Spiritual Diary this week as you begin to know and express the Truth about your divine connection. Continue to ask yourself the all-important question, "In what ways am I now unfolding?"

Remember always that you are divinely connected to God and the universe. In and through all things this wonderful flow of love and good continues without pause or break, constantly strengthening and sustaining all.

Pattern Two

Lesson 4

Dear Student:

During the first three lessons of this Pattern you have concentrated your efforts on experiencing God in the world. The discovery that beauty is everywhere, and the experience of beauty as an elevating feeling, lead naturally to the perception that what pervades the world is absolutely good. This something is recognized as God.

God is not a being or person having life, intelligence, love, power. God is that invisible, intangible (but very real) something we call life. God is perfect love and infinite power. God is the total of these, the total of all good, whether manifested or unexpressed.

111

There is but one God in the universe,
but one source of all the different forms
of life or intelligence that we see, whether they be men, animals, trees, or rocks
(H. Emilie Cady, Lessons in Truth).

When awareness of the limitless accessi-
bility of God begins to expand your thought
and experience, you recognize a divine connection between yourself and God. You are
blessed as you become more open and receptive to the constant flow of God's love and
good to you and through you, and as you
begin to perceive ever more clearly that this
divine connection unites everything in the
universe!

PATTERN TWO

Learning to Reach Out

Lesson 4: Oneness

You have arrived at the conclusion that
God is *immanent* in the world. That is, He is
manifested or expressed in the empirical,
sensible world. God exists and operates within
all things. He is inherent in the universe. Yet
in another sense, you also perceive that God is

transcendent. He is somehow above all things, beyond ordinary limits, exceeding all knowledge and surpassing all material existence. He is more wonderful, more beautiful than appearances in the universe. It is possible to "see God" in nature, but when you approach the perception of God in the world—God as form—you feel at once that the awareness of God is also greater, much more beautiful, and more magnificent than your physical senses can comprehend. You also see that God is formless.

Although this beautiful world seems to suggest and hint at God in every way, you feel that God also exists as unmanifested Spirit. You feel God very near, even obvious to you when you look for Him, yet at the same time He is beyond all appearances. He is in and through all things, yet somehow transcends the physical universe.

You behold nature in a constant state of generation and degeneration, of never-ending growth and change. Yet in the midst of all this change, there exists the idea of God as changeless—the one fixed point of all existence. God stands somehow beyond the universe, yet is also immanent and accessible to you when you are centered in Him. It seems to be a strange paradox that God is transcendent, yet also close at hand, but you have already worked with this paradox and have begun to solve it in the context of your own experience.

Earlier you read that "there is but one Source of being." This statement implies that in God, all things come and go, all else is changeable and inconstant. Only God is changeless, immutable Being.

In prayer we need to be deeply conscious that God is the almighty One, the supreme Creator and ruler of the universe, that He is infinite and eternal; we need to know that God is the underlying, unchangeable Truth, "with whom can be no variation, neither shadow that is cast by turning" *(Charles Fillmore, Keep a True Lent).*

Let your thoughts be directed to this idea: *God is the almighty One.*

He is the one Source of all there is, the one criterion for all knowledge, the one power, the one presence in the universe. This vast world of countless upon countless forms and phases of life exists within that One. That

One alone is without beginning or end, without a second, without variation.

God is the one fixed point of the universe. When your mind and heart are centered in God, your fixed point of reference, all else in your life falls into right perspective. If you were to draw a circle with a compass, and if you kept the point centered in one fixed place, the circumference would be a perfect circle. All phases of your life demonstrate perfect wholeness, perfect guidance and direction when you are perfectly fixed within, in God.

As you come into the awareness that "God is the underlying, unchangeable Truth," a feeling of unity with all other seekers of Truth begins to grow in your understanding. You realize that although each individual who reads and studies Truth has a unique and personal way of thinking about God, there is something *alike* something that is shared in the experience of Truth. Whether your name for God is the Lord, the Christ, Divine Mind, Supreme Being, Heavenly Father, Vishnu, Shiva, Krishna, Zoroaster, Allah, Buddha, or any other name for the deity you address in worship, the experience of peace and oneness that comes in prayer is an experience accessible to all persons. Regardless of the method, regardless of the time and place, God is available to all, to each. This experience is of equal

magnitude and effect no matter what approach is taken. There are many ways to get to the roof of a house, but whether you use a ladder or a rope or a stairway, the goal is the same. Because this world is of God and in God, all ways lead to Him. Thinking of this diagram may help you to reach this realization:

When an individual has reached this realization, surface differences tend to dissolve. The effects of his spiritual understanding are evident in his very presence. Seeing such a person, people may disagree about his age, they may disagree about his nationality or his social class, but all will readily agree that he is *unusual.* They sense that he is "close to God"; they will say, "Here is a holy man."

Something happens to conversation, to events, when he is present. Those who are near him feel lifted, blessed, spiritually "refreshed." Somehow his words, looks, gestures affect those around him. They feel their thoughts turning from conflict to peace, from fear to courage, from sickness to health, from weakness to strength, from hate to love, from death to eternal life.

Such a person has discovered what you can

discover. He has found the one fixed point of the universe, the ultimate goal to which all roads lead, the one Source from which all things come, and in which all things exist. This realization that God is One unifies and blesses all experience.

Any religion or religious philosophy may have apparent weaknesses and inconsistencies, yet the love of God and the earnest desire to reach Him overcome all else. If a man has several children, the older may call him "father," while the babies can only say "dada." Still, the father knows that each is calling him, and he comes to whichever child calls. By whatever name you call God, by whatever method of prayer you use to reach the awareness of Him, give that method all your attention, complete faith and love, your most diligent and sincere effort, and surely *you will reach God.*

When you realize that all paths lead to God, you know that He is here, present in all things. He is around you just as the very air is around you. All people (consciously or unconsciously) are seeking Him, for all the life and ceaseless activity of the universe is actually a restlessness to reach oneness with God.

You may wish to reread this part of Pattern Two several times this week. No doubt, each time you will add to it from your own thought and experience to attain increasing understanding of oneness with God.

Practice Exercise

Instructions: For review of past practice exercises and in order to gain a sense of relationship in your lessons, a separate exercise is given for each day of the week.

1st day: The practice exercise given in Pattern One, Lesson 1, marked a beginning in your life. It was a kind of declaration of your freedom from all bondage of time. By this realization you are consecrated and dedicated in God's name. Reread and practice this exercise once again. Then return to this page.

The exercise seems simple enough, yet now more than before you begin to experience the full impact of the idea of freedom from all limitation of time. You know that because God is all, you live and move in God's good time.

Become still for a moment, and as you retain this wonderful feeling of freedom, affirm with new faith and understanding:

I am one with God.

2d day: Read and practice the exercise at the close of Pattern One, Lesson 2. Then turn back to this page.

You know that, in truth, you are eternal, free spirit. As you feel your body and mind in perfect accord, you know that you are in tune with the infinite power and love of God that pervades the universe. You are filled with God's perfect rhythm and harmony. Your every body function, your every thought and feeling are blessed by the harmonizing, revitalizing activity of God. He sings His song of life through you. Affirm with thanksgiving:

I am one with God.

3d day: Thoughtfully review the practice exercise in Pattern One, Lesson 3 before continuing with your exercise today.

Peace, be still. You are now centered within, in perfect strength, perfect peace. You are building a foundation of experience and understanding that, like the strong, immovable tower of your imagination, can never be shaken. You have discovered that God exists in the midst of you as changeless, eternal Spirit. This discovery is the key to spirituality. Know for yourself:

120

I am one with God.

4th day: Today, read and study again the practice exercise included in Pattern One, Lesson 4.

The light of God's love within you guides, blesses, and protects you. This same light surrounds and illumines the universe. As you recognize the radiance of God's love shining in and through you, you are filled with light, love, and peace. Know that the whole world is filled with that same light, love, and peace. In joy and love affirm:

I am one with God.

5th day: Turn back to the first practice exercise of Pattern Two. Study and follow it before resuming your work today.

The ideal of followers of many religions has been ultimately to live in some kind of heaven with God. Now as you look lovingly and creatively around you, you see that right now, you live in paradise, for you see God manifested as beauty and order everywhere. As you dwell in this feeling of loving appreciation, affirm:

I am one with God.

6th day: Now you are ready to read again the practice exercise included in Pattern Two,

121

Lesson 2. When you have carefully followed the exercise, turn back to this page.

When you look for the good in life, and when you are open and ready in mind and heart to accept God's infinite blessings, you feel a flood of great joy within you. You actively and lovingly reach out with your whole being to meet the wonderful promise of every day. God's abundant good is ever available to you, as you acknowledge this truth:

I am one with God.

7th day: Review the Pattern Two, Lesson 3 practice exercise. By now you feel your experiencing leading you to the conclusion that you are divinely connected to God.

You know that God is the one Source of being, constantly extending to you all good, all life, all love, all wisdom, and all power. When you let go of all negative and limiting thoughts and feelings, and when you actively reach out with your mind and heart to God, you become an open, receptive channel for God's limitless good. With a great new understanding of unity, acknowledge for yourself:

I am one with God.

The notes you add this week in your Spiri-

122

tual Diary are a priceless source of recording and evaluating your own spiritual unfoldment. Compare the notes you have made on your practice exercises this week with those made earlier in your study. Already you have made great strides!

Your experiences in these past weeks have led you to understand that God is both immanent and transcendent. You no longer need to look forward to a nebulous future when God will appear in the world and all will somehow be made right, for now when you follow your higher understanding, you cannot *help* but see God in everyone you meet, in every article of the everyday. Differences and conflict, paradox and argument, all fade away in the light of this great unifying experience. God is everywhere, indicating His presence to you in countless ways. Think of these many ways as you keep your Spiritual Diary, and never fail to ask yourself, "In what ways am I now unfolding?" As you study and pray, know always that God is within you, immediate and close as your all-knowing, all-loving Teacher, protecting and guiding you to your highest good.

In each of the various approaches given in

these two Patterns you have reached a sense of oneness with God. As you prepare to go on to Pattern Three, this new understanding blesses you and leads you to many wonderful things to come.

Pattern Three

Lesson 1

Dear Student:

In the last pattern, you began to gain a new sense of wholeness and fulfillment. The broken pieces of life begin to fall together for you in a related pattern of experience. It is no longer necessary to concentrate on dividing the ugly from the beautiful, or the good from the bad in appearances, for in and through it all a higher pattern emerges. There is inherent goodness and infinite possibility in every atom of the universe. Life is not so imperfect, after all. There is much more to it than you had imagined, and it is much better than you thought.

No mere philosophical rationalization could have contained this understanding for you; it could not have been handed to you in a tidy package of wisdom, because you had to experience it for yourself. Logical deduction is helpful in learning about Truth; it is clear and logical that if God is all, and all is good, then God is good. But until these statements are real in your own experience, they have little value to you. You have had to make an active interchange—a subtle but stimulating trade of old ways of thinking for new ideas. But you know that this continuous process is life-giving. Bless you as you actively and joyously continue in spiritual unfoldment!

PATTERN THREE

Learning to Look Inward

Lesson 1: Identifying Yourself

You have learned that appearances are limited and limiting, but that Truth gives freedom from all limitations. There is no need to feel entangled by the concept of time; no need to let apparent disharmony, disunity, or darkness in the world keep you in constant bondage. Instead, you need merely to reach out for reality. You need to reach out for the

126

goodness and beauty of life that is everywhere and accept it freely and joyously, knowing that God is the one Source of all good, the one Presence and Power in the universe.

The recognition of the Truth that God is omnipotent and omnipresent leads you to the conclusion that God alone exists as all-pervading, infinite consciousness. This is an inspiring, freeing statement of Truth, but you might feel somewhat "lost" in it right now. Where in this all-pervading Spirit is the "you" that eats and sleeps and thinks and reads this page? Although your thinking logically leads you to assume that if God is all, then there is really no division, no separation, for life is actually a manifestation of that One, you may feel somehow outside, looking in at this spiritual cosmology. You may ask, "Where do I find *myself* . . . where and who or what am I?"

If you consult your mirror for the answer to this question, you could at once say, "I am man or woman, of such and such an age, brown-eyed, hazel-eyed, blue-eyed, dark- or light-skinned, round or thin, straight-haired, curly-haired, tall or short," and so on and on. But you find the thought creeping in, "I am this—but I am *much more* than this, too."

Something looks out of your eyes that is more than brown or hazel or blue, more than the result of a curious arrangement of chromosomes, more than age or sex, tall or short, light or dark. You know that you are more than so many pounds of flesh, bone, nerves, and tissue. You have a way of speaking about the physical parts of you as "my hands, my feet, my shoulder, my eyes, my heart," as if to declare that there is something about you beyond the physical that is the possessor of these many parts, the real essence of what you are. You know already without being told that something about you transcends your physical self. And so the question comes again, "Who am I really; what is my real identity?"

The very fact that you have the ability to question and to wonder indicates another aspect of you. You are a mental, as well as a physical, being. You have the ability to imagine, to choose, to interpret, to will. You express your mental self in all that you do as you constantly mold and translate your world with your every thought. In every way, you leave traces of yourself.

If you search for clues to your identity among these traces, you perhaps find a stack of documents which apparently testify to your identity. Here is a birth certificate; here are various licenses, diplomas, deeds, documents to signify ownership, business transactions, loans, promises, and several other papers and cards which together say, "This person has this name, was born at this time and place, has this level of intelligence and achievement, owns such and such and is responsible for this or that."

But is there not still more to you than all of this? With all of these papers before you, would you not think, "I have really lived more than all of this can show; I have felt more, loved more, thought more, and dreamed more than is recorded here"? These seem to be mere "fingerprints" of yours. Your real thoughts and dreams reach far beyond them. In the marvelous mental faculty of imagination, you can evade time completely, travel faster than the speed of light, pass all distance, and overcome all appearances. Your mind can grasp the dualities of this finite world and yet go beyond, to a sense of the infinite, the changeless, the nonrelative. This is true because something within you is itself changeless and nonrelative. This transcends the physical you and the mental you. It supersedes the "personal" you altogether—it is what you really are.

When you identify yourself solely with the personal, you are not satisfied. There is a lack for which you cannot account, but which is very real to you . . . Knowing the personal, only, you have but a superficial knowledge of yourself. Beneath the surface the rich deeps of life summon you with over-mastering appeal. . . .

The personal, the *who* can be changed. You have changed it many times and you will continue to change it . . . The *what* is not affected. That is changeless. It eternally will be what it eternally has been. It is the divinity of which Peter said in a moment of insight, "Thou art the . . . Son of the living God" *(Imelda O. Shanklin, What Are You?).*

When you look into a mirror, you do not see this true Self that is the real you. But when you learn to look for the eternal good that is there, that real Self shines forth in your every thought and act. In last week's study you began to see beyond a negative perception of the world to its inherent goodness and beauty, to the recognition that God is everywhere present, in all things. Now you will begin to behold yourself in a spiritual light as you really are, a perfect child of God.

According to an old story, a great king awoke one morning to find that his memory of who or what he was had vanished completely. Although he still wore the golden crown, he had forgotten his identity. The one person in all the kingdom who could tell him who he was, he reasoned, should be the ruler of the land who must indeed know everything. But of course, he sought the king in vain, for he himself was the very man for whom he searched. He looked throughout the city, but to no avail. Discouraged, he wandered into the forest, still unable to find anyone who could solve his mystery. Days passed until finally, overcome with exhaustion and thirst, he fell down beside a pool of water. When he leaned over the shining pool, he caught a glimpse of his image reflected there. When he saw the golden crown on his head, his memory at once returned and he said, "I

131

myself am the king!"

Think how *you* are like the king in this story. You search everywhere for the answer to the question, "Who am I?"—you look everywhere for the clues to your real spiritual identity, when all along, the answer is right within yourself. You must learn to look within your own being for that shining true Self. When you behold that which you have been seeking, you realize that each person is, in truth, "spiritual royalty." You know that it is possible for each person to exercise spiritual dominion over his life and thought. You may then know the truth about yourself, and say, "Here, within me, is the King Himself!"

This is the wonderful, transforming recognition that within the apparent you exists the eternal, perfect expression of God. Despite your many disguises, the truth about you is never altogether hidden. Within you in the midst of all change, apart and watchful of the constant drama and suspense of life, is that ever-shining Self. Throughout your every activity, that Self is present. Whether you be awake or asleep, at work or resting, angry or loving, patient or impatient, that pure Self waits within you for expression. This higher

Self, this ever-perfect central part of your being, has been called the indwelling Christ.*

*Christ, indwelling—The Son of God or spiritual nucleus within each person. All our thoughts must harmonize with this spiritual center before we can bring into expression the divine consciousness. Each man has within himself the Christ idea, just as Jesus had. Man must look to the indwelling Christ in order to recognize his sonship, his divine origin and birth, even as did the Savior. This real self is "closer . . . than breathing, and nearer than hands and feet." It is the kingdom of God in each person. "Neither shall they say, Lo, here! or, There! for lo, the kingdom of God is within you" *(Charles Fillmore, The Revealing Word).*

As you read once more the definition given above, you know that these words are Truth, relevant to you today, right now. You can scarcely read the quotation from Luke without a kind of thrill, as you begin to recognize that the kingdom of God *is* within you. The indwelling Christ is ready at this moment to fulfill your every need. When you read these

133

words, your concentration begins to be directed within you. It is as if your thoughts point inward to the answer to the mystery of your true identity. This is what you are; here is the golden crown of your divinity; here within you is the kingdom of God.

This Self has been called the "spiritual nucleus within each person." You know that the nucleus of any living cell is the starting point, the source of all growth, the seed containing all power for the ultimate plan of expression. Consider that your Christ Self is your own source of power, of growth, your own ultimate spiritual expression. It is this awareness for which you are always reaching, consciously or unconsciously.

Read once more the line of Tennyson's poetry that Charles Fillmore quoted in his definition above: "closer . . . than breathing, and nearer than hands and feet." Listen now to the soft, even sound of your own breathing as you read. Know that back of even this most vital activity exists that perfect Self— immutable and constant, radiating perfect love. This Self is "nearer than hands and feet." When you think of these words, your mind is directed away from the outer aspects of your life, inward even from your physical body, to that spiritual center within you.

As you go on to the practice exercise, let this inward tendency of your thoughts continue. Consciously bring your thinking and feeling into harmony with that center within you. Learn to identify yourself with the Christ within.

Practice Exercise

Bring a small mirror with you to your study place. Lesson Three is focused on self-discovery, and so this mirror will be used as an aid to seeing yourself as you really are in this exercise.

Read through the practice exercise each day this week, then put aside your lesson and practice it. Remember that you have set the personal goal of working on your exercise for fifteen minutes each day. By this daily activity you are reminding yourself of your purpose of spiritual growth. You are daily affirming your spiritual identity.

Step 1. Hold your mirror before you and look carefully at your image. When you see the reflection, you instantly recognize it as your own. Here is the face that has looked back at you from mirrors all your life. The passing of time, loss or gain of body weight, or perhaps changes in hair style have altered your appearance somewhat but, after all, you are somehow the same. You know that something about you is a constant factor. Your identity has a changeless base.

Immediately your mind may begin to evaluate your reflection. Almost impulsively you turn your face from side to side. You can hardly resist smoothing an eyebrow or patting a hair into place. "Is that a wrinkle or a shadow?" you might think, or, "Should I make some changes, a new way of combing my hair, perhaps?" Do not condemn yourself for what seems to be nothing more than vanity, but rather think in this way: all this is really the tendency of your mind to seek perfection. Let go of all thoughts of self-criticism, and know that the perfection you seek is not here in the outer reflection of you, but closer, nearer. Perfection exists within you as your Christ Self, eternally beautiful and peaceful.

Step 2. Put down your mirror for a moment now, and close your eyes. Turn all of your thoughts deep within. Affirm quietly,

I acknowledge the indwelling Christ.

Say the words once more, slowly and thoughtfully. Your thoughts will cease to point outward to the physical you. All worry and confusion slip away as your thoughts seek inner direction. The Christ within you peacefully stills your body and mind. Here within your own being, beyond all change and appearances exists your quiet, shining, perfect Self. In this realization, speak aloud these words:

I acknowledge the indwelling Christ as my true Self.

Consciously hold this thought with all the force of your being. As you begin more and more to accept the Truth of your affirmation, repeat the words silently once again:

I acknowledge the indwelling Christ as my true Self.

Step 3. Now, look again into your mirror. You will at once notice a new radiance in your face. Your expression is now peaceful and happy as the radiance of the indwelling Christ is reflected in your smile. A new poise and beauty shines in your face, for you have discovered the true source of beauty within you.

As you keep your Spiritual Diary, ask yourself: "What is my real nature? How do I identify myself?" And reflect, "In what ways am I now unfolding?"

In all your activities, look for and give thanks for every evidence of your true nature, your Christ nature. Choose not to dwell on thoughts of self-criticism, but rather to dwell with your whole mind and heart on your own indwelling Christ. Whenever you see your reflection, look for your true Self shining in your face. In every way, acknowledge the indwelling Christ as your true Self, guiding you to ever greater joy and understanding through this and the lessons ahead!

Pattern Three

Lesson 2

Dear Student:

Even though you began this series of lessons some time ago, you know that this way of life is really made up of beginnings. While you have a sense of growing, of becoming, you also know that there is no end or limit to the Truth that awaits you. The ideas you have recognized as Truth and that you have begun to apply in your thinking and living have already brought an entirely new direction to your life. What may have started as a kind of curiosity has become a genuine longing to know and express God.

Keep the sense of joy, of new beginning, and know that you are helped and sustained by prayer!

PATTERN THREE

Learning to Look Inward

Lesson 2: Turning Inward

In your course work in Pattern Two, you found that although the world is full or apparent dualities, contradiction, and contrast, God exists in and through all things as unchanging, unifying presence. You know that if you look out the window right now and see that a terrific storm is raging, you would not say that the storm is the very essence, or the central fact, of the world, for you know that the world exists throughout a thousand different moods of changing weather and seasons. Thunder and lightning are among the moods of nature, as are sunshine and soft breezes. Whatever it is that is manifested as so much change must itself be changeless. That which undergoes growth and decay is itself birthless, deathless, decayless. Bring this conclusion into relationship with the mystery of your own identity.

If you become very nervous, you still would not say that nervousness is the natural state of your being, for you know that while at one time you may be very upset, at another time you have a calm, peaceful attitude. You change your mood thousands of times, just as you might change your hat and coat, and still you do not change yourself. Just as none of the various moods of nature represents the ultimate truth about the world, the passing moods and changes in your attitude do not represent your true self. When you experience resentment, you do not say, "I am resentment," but perhaps, "I *feel* resentment." You are acknowledging the truth that your attitude or mood is a passing thing. It affects you, yet it is separate from you.

You go through life, shopping for attitudes, for understanding, as if you were shopping for clothes. You try on one garment of thought after another, keeping one for a while, then casting it aside. Somehow you are dissatisfied with those that do not "become" you; you search for something that expresses your "better self."

This vague feeling of dissatisfaction that seems to accompany the human condition must also be cast aside. This sense of emptiness, loss, or separation no longer suits you when you accept yourself as you really are, for you know that the highest beauty and Truth lie right within you. This Christ within can never be lost.

It is not something extra that has been added to the physical, mental you. Rather, it is the ultimate self of you to which all your other attributes have been added. These characteristics that make up the personal you may either hide or express the Truth of your being. But whether your true self is hidden or revealed in your life is really your own choice.

You must learn to make this choice according to the Truth you have learned by constantly analyzing your mood, your way of thinking. If this mood is not in accordance with your ideal, if it is gloom, insecurity, fear, or anger, make up your mind to transform this mood to happiness, strength, courage, love.

This careful discipline of thought and word leads to a definite change in your attitude toward yourself. As this attitude changes, you free your own inner potential. You open your mind and your life to the expression of God within you. The results in your life are powerful!

What you believe about religion,

philosophy, science, people, things—all these beliefs color your life. But what you believe about yourself is most important of all, because you can never be anything else but yourself, and what you believe about everything else is closely related to what you believe about yourself.

. . . What you become is also the result of your belief in yourself, in God in you, in soul power which is His very special gift to you, capable of infinite possibilities of good, capable of overcoming limitations that may seem very real to you: illness, handicaps, poverty, loneliness, ineffectiveness. You can do anything needful or desirable through the power that is within you, if only you stir up that power into activity *(Ernest Wilson, Soul Power)*.

Your own "soul power," the Christ within you, is beyond all limits of personality or appearances. It is an outpicturing of God within you through which all things are possible. No disease or handicap can hold you, for you are perfect and whole in the sight of God. No poverty can hold you, for you inherit

God's endless bounty. Loneliness cannot hold you, for you are in eternal unity with all life. No apparent ineffectiveness can hold you, for infinite ability, creativity, strength and purpose are your real nature. Through Christ within you, you are powerful to do all things.

You now recognize the fact that your true self is ever perfect, changeless, ever shining at the center of your being. The outer you is constantly subject to changes of all kinds, but the inner you is unalterable, pure Spirit. Study again the definition of Spirit given in your first week of study:

> Spirit, our innermost, real being, the absolute part of us, the *I* of us, has never changed, though our thoughts and our circumstances may have changed hundreds of times. This part of us is a standing forth of God into visibility *(H. Emilie Cady, Lessons in Truth).*

When you realize this truth, you know it is not accurate to say of yourself, "I am weak," for at the core of your being is unfailing, dynamic, measureless power. You must never say, "I am foolish," for at the center of your being is all the wisdom of the universe. You are never "unattractive," for the indwelling

144

Christ is the most attractive and attracting force in existence.

Whenever you speak of yourself, guard against this kind of mislabeling. Remember always your true identity. When you catch yourself saying that you are in some way inadequate or worthless, remind yourself of what you know to be true.

Learn to stand as a witness to your thoughts and feelings. There are two basic justifications for this mental activity: one, you learn to judge for yourself whether or not your thinking conforms to the standards of right belief and right attitude you have set; two, you learn that the abnegating process you applied in learning to see the world as it really is must also be applied in seeing yourself as *you* really are.

If you look into the bowl of a spoon at your own reflection, you know that you do not look at all like the blurred, distorted image you see there. If the image you hold of yourself in your mind is blurred and distorted, remember that this too is unreal. You must readjust your thinking to see clearly and truly. Right now, in the secret of your own mind and heart, prepare to adjust your inner vision to see yourself in the true way—to behold God within you.

"Pray to thy Father who is in secret." In the hidden recesses of your own soul, you will find wondrous things—the courage, the inspiration, and the joy you are seeking. There, in the place of adjustment, you will discover the magic mirror in which the true self is reflected as the image and likeness of the Creator *(Richard Lynch, Know Thyself)*.

If you find yourself saying or thinking that you are poor, weak, foolish, or sinful, immediately correct these thoughts by means of mental denial. Say to yourself, "I am neither poor, weak, foolish, nor sinful, for my true self, the indwelling Christ, is rich in infinite supply, infinitely powerful, wise, and pure."

Know that your divine inheritance is unlimited abundance, complete wholeness and happiness, perfect oneness with God. Remove the false beliefs that have colored your self-perception as you would remove an old coat. If you find that the coat you are wearing is tattered and grimy, you remove it and get rid of it. In the same way, if you discover that the attitudes and beliefs you hold do not

146

reflect your high ideal, you cast them off. They do not "become" you, for they do not help you to become a truer reflection and expression of the glory within you.

Renounce all belief that you are "sinful"— believe in your innate purity. Refuse to believe in your weakness; believe in your strength. Let go of unhappiness, cling to joy. Release the mental hold you have on limitation, lack, suffering, and hold instead with all your might to your spiritual nature.

As long as you hold in your mind the feeling of separation from God, you hold back from your life infinite blessings and fulfillment. As long as you are convinced that God is somewhere "out there," you will never find peace. But when you point to your own inner self and know, "God is here," you find peace.

Practice Exercise

Sit with spine straight, both feet on the floor, and begin to direct your thoughts inward. Use your will to still your body; turn away demands of your senses and look inward, to know and accept the indwelling Christ as your perfect self. Affirm:

I turn within to the Christ in me.

Now close your eyes and repeat the affirmation slowly and with purpose. Begin to think of all the attributes of the indwelling Christ: perfect strength, infinite wisdom, love, and power. Here is the source of healing, the light of right guidance, the magnet of all good. You begin to feel that you are filled with peace, perfect peace.

Pause now to let your whole being become enfolded in this perfect peace. Do not try to hurry—the experience will come. It is beginning now.

The diagram below may be helpful to you

in turning within. Imagine you are looking from the point of the cone outward to the circumference of the base. This is the way man most often looks at the world. The outer appearances, the circumference of life gets the most attention. From this viewpoint, life seems to be a constantly whirling activity with no center of stillness, no fixed point of reference.

Close your eyes for a moment and imagine this cone slowly turning toward you so that you may look inward, to the apex. Pause now and actually visualize the cone opening to you.

This mental picture can give form and direction to your thinking as you use it with the purpose of looking into the very center of your own being. Establish in your mind that you are not merely contemplating a form, but actually *forming your thoughts* toward a central reference point.

This is not mere "mental gymnastics," but actually is an effective method of centering your thoughts on the one fixed point in your life—the indwelling Christ. Here is the shining self of you, here is the light beyond all change and death. Acknowledge this with the statement:

*I turn within to the center of my being;
here is perfect bliss, perfect peace.*

In this way you begin to transfer your consciousness from the finite world to the infinite. Although God can be perceived as immanent in all creation, and though you feel the harmony and vitality of His life flowing through your physical body, great release and wisdom lie in perceiving your own eternal self as beyond all form and finite limits. Think that your mind is going from movement to stillness, from the outside of you to the inside, from the unreal to the real.

If at any time appearances begin to convince you that you are less than you really are, use this image of the cone to bring your thoughts into right focus. Deliberately withdraw your attention from externals in order to focus on your inner source of Truth. When you contemplate the mental image of the cone, think of all your thoughts traveling inward, away from all external distractions and concerns, away from the physical you who bears such and such a name and lives in such and such conditions.

Know that you are that center of pure light

within you. You are that source of perfect health, peace, abundance, power, love, and happiness. You are that Christ within.

Remember to write down your own thoughts and experiences in your Spiritual Diary. This is an activity you will probably want to take up very often. On some days you may feel that thoughts and experiences that you want to record come to you in such a concentrated way that you need to pick up your Diary and write in it several times a day. On other days, you may seem to be quietly assimilating what you are learning, and may not feel the need to write. But remember that keeping your notes and recording your own responses to the material is a vital part of your growth. As you think and grow, always consider, "In what ways am I now unfolding?" By this method you reinforce your understanding of the principles given in the course material, and you build a helpful, enlightening record of your own personal and spiritual unfoldment. As you await Lesson 3 of this pattern, you are gaining in the love, the joy, and the realization of Truth.

Pattern Three
Lesson 3

Dear Student:

Remember that at the outset of your study, you consecrated and dedicated your chosen study place in God's name. Now you can feel truly at home here—this is your own spiritual laboratory, cleansed and prepared for great discoveries. Here is a climate for spiritual growth.

As you undertake this lesson, be uplifted and receptive to the realization that, in reality, all the world has a spiritual climate; all of life is an opportunity to know and live your highest ideals!

PATTERN THREE

Learning to Look Inward

Lesson 3: Reaching Inward

By this time you begin to feel that you can easily and naturally turn within, just as you felt the cone image turning toward you in your mind to guide your thoughts inward. You begin to feel the pull of inner direction—you know you are on the right track. All of your studies thus far have actually been leading your mind in this direction. Even when you were apparently reaching outward with your perception, you were really learning to perceive things from within yourself. Now instead of feeling that outer events control you, or that outer conditions act upon you directly to affect your life, you are learning to observe appearances "indirectly" through your own innate higher perception and understanding. You know that you are not merely a pawn in life, but that by this inner leading you receive right guidance and act with strength of purpose.

You are beginning to see yourself less and less in relation only to the uncertainties, the changing moods and phases of life. Instead you can see yourself in relation to God within you.

There comes to be in this sweet and holy relation a living touch, an intimate sort of interspheoring of our whole being with the divine source of all good and all giving. We become conscious of a new relationship between the living, indwelling Christ, unto whom is given all power, and the creature whose needs are unlimited. . . . You get to know that the infinite supply for soul, body, and circumstances is someway right at hand in the indwelling Christ *(H. Emilie Cady, God a Present Help)*.

Read the quotation above once more, thoughtfully and carefully. Think about the words *living touch.* These two words alone place the experience the author describes far beyond the level of speculation or cold theory. This is no fantasy or mental delirium; the realization of this sweet and holy relation between you and the indwelling Christ is real, dynamic, transforming. Reaching within to contact your higher self is a living and intimate experience. It is an experience that goes

154

beyond intellectualization; it supersedes the material, sensible universe. It is so complete and wonderful that it exceeds all power of description.

Yet throughout the history of religious literature, writers have used sensual images to explain spiritual experience. They may say that it is like the sense of hearing, but clearer than the physical ear can detect. They may say it is like touching or tasting, but more acute. They may say it is like a profound sleep, yet infinitely more restful and peaceful. Or they may say it is like an awakening, but more renewing and revitalizing. They may say it is like being born, yet all admit that this spiritual contact or rebirth opens the way to an awareness of life more vivid and real than any preceding perception could contain. This use of metaphor upon metaphor in every body of scripture ever compiled is clear testimony that religious experience transcends all other experience.

If you think it wonderful to touch a soft, full rose, or the warm earth, or the side of your own face, or the hand of one you love who loves you, know that this living touch between you and your own inner self is yet

155

more wonderful than all of these. This thrill is lasting, freeing, comforting, enfolding, illuminating. This is, after all, the true goal of all your prayer, all your striving, all your living. This is the perfect pearl that a wise man sells all his other possessions to buy. This is the source of infinite supply for every phase of your life, every moment of your life. It is your inexhaustible treasure.

Yet it is not possible for this inner treasure to be hoarded or contained. When you free this "divine source of all good and all giving" in your mind and life, you find that it is the nature of the Christ within to shine forth to uplift you and all those around you—to transform your life in every good way. You will experience a joy much greater than if you had been given the greatest treasure on earth; an experience of satisfaction beyond words; an intersphering of your whole being more fulfilling even than falling in love, more profound and moving than any worldly wisdom.

Yet as transcendent as this inner communion with God appears, it is also the most practical, productive, physically and mentally renewing experience possible. God is knowable and present in and through your life.

In the quotation from *God a Present Help*, the author explains that the indwelling Christ is "right at hand." When something is right at hand, it is instantly within your experience. Think how very close God is to you.

If you touch your wrist with your hand, you notice with what immeasurable speed the message of sense contact is relayed to your brain center. Each time you try it, you will be impressed with the immediacy of sense perception, with the wonder of your body. With every beat of your pulse, every cell growth or movement, every electric nerve signal, the concentrated life force of God is in constant, living activity. God within you is the Observer of all your experiences, the silent Knower behind all your thoughts.

Beyond and behind all perception, the indwelling Christ is right at hand within you. If there were a coarse, heavy piece of cloth over your wrist you might not be able to feel the touch of your hand with the same clarity and quickness. So it is that if your mind is covered by false notions and muffled by confusing thoughts, you cannot so clearly perceive the living presence of the Christ within you.

Yet that presence is unfailing. That light of

157

eternal peace and wisdom shines within you at all times. However limiting appearances in your life may seem, remember the indwelling Christ is responsive to your every need. God within you hears each prayer, and answers in the still small voice.

God is the "still small voice" in every soul that heals and blesses and up-lifts. . . .

That "still small voice" at the center of our being does not command what we shall be or what we shall do or not do. It is so gentle and still in its work that in the hurly-burly of life we overlook it entirely. . . .

Compared with audible language, communion in mind can be said to be without sound. It is the "still small voice," the voice that is not a voice, the voice using words that are not words. Yet its language is more definite and certain than that of words and sounds, because it has none of their limita-tions. . . . It is your natural language *(Charles Fillmore, Jesus Christ Heals).*

Pause for a moment and let your mind rest in these ideas. Speak the words:

*God is the still small voice within me
that heals, blesses, and uplifts me.*

Think of a wonderfully beautiful voice speaking from within you in clear, gentle tones, saying to you now:

You are healed, blessed, and uplifted.

In your mind, you can hear the sound of the voice. You can hear it pause after each word. As you listen again to the affirmation you can feel your whole being healed in every part, blessed in every way, uplifted to the joy and freedom of Spirit.

To get a definite, personal idea of what the still small voice is like, it may help you to think of that same voice speaking to you in the words of this lesson. When you mentally listen to it, think that it is your own personal, inner Teacher, gently answering your every question, leading you to an ever deeper understanding of Truth. Think how it is like the voice of your higher self.

The still small voice that speaks to you is not a stern, condemning voice, but is completely gentle and comforting, guiding you lovingly in all things. It teaches you the Truth of your own being, that you are eternal, free spirit.

When you concentrate on the spiritual center within you, you are opening the way in your mind and heart to receive the guidance and inspiration of the still small voice. When you reach within to the indwelling Christ, you begin to perceive with increasing clarity God's living message.

Perhaps this inner voice is called "still" because in contrast to all the movement and ceaseless change in life, it represents a fixed point, ultimate stillness and peace. It is called "small," for it seems so insignificant in life's turmoil. This most precious source is completely unpretentious; you must listen for it with great care and patience. You must reach for it with great zeal and determination. But when you do begin to hear the still small voice, it is in the way of a calm knowing, an uplifting inspiration, new-found strength and purpose, and an infilling of peace.

When you hear this inner voice of Spirit, you may not hear actual words. But the answers you seek to life are not really in words. Think of the answers you have received that came in a pause between words, or in a single look or gesture, or in a sunset, a falling leaf, or a rose. Language is a way in which life's messages are encoded. Yet when you hear the still small voice, you receive your messages in a more direct way. Words and languages are relative; that inner self is nonrelative. The "language" of Spirit is called "your natural language," because it is of your true self, and all Truth, all power, all healing is natural to that indwelling Christ.

But in order to be attuned to this inner voice, you must listen intently with your thoughts and feelings. Remember that in Lesson 2, you found that to seek the good inherent in your surroundings, you need to let your whole mind become involved in a reaching activity. As portrayed in the Michelangelo painting of the hand of God reaching to touch the hand of man, seeking God is a double reaching activity. God reaches out to you from everywhere, even from within your very being. You must add to this your own reaching in mind and heart to join spiritually with God, the focal point of Spirit within you.

This is the point in every man where God joins hands with him. . . . It is here that man understands what it is to be inspired by the Spirit to say and do things extraordinary in the sight of the world *(Charles Fillmore, Talks on Truth).*

The experience you seek *is* extraordinary in the context of life as it appears, and its effects in your life are extraordinary. Yet in the understanding that life is really a spiritual activity, and that you—eternal, free spirit—live, move, and have your being in God, the good, you accept the experience of inner communion with Him as the most completely "ordinary" and natural experience in life. Although preparing yourself to receive inner guidance may at first seem to be a rigorous and difficult task, remember that the Christ within you is near and accessible. As you reach inward, God is reaching out to you.

Practice Exercise

Begin your exercise with constructive mental denials and affirmations. You must redirect any negative activities of thought or action in positive ways. Look over the following sets of affirmations and denials; then give each pair of statements careful thought. Think of the ideas expressed in relation to your own life and consciousness. Repeat the statements with the power of your own will behind them. Give them all the emphasis you can. By this method you turn your thought power away from that which is destructive and limiting and direct your thoughts to infinite good.

I do not reach out for imperfection and ugliness in the world around me—
I reach inward to the eternal beauty and goodness of the indwelling Christ.

I do not reach out for doubts and confusion—
I reach inward to God's infinite wisdom and harmony.

I do not reach out for pain or sickness in my physical being—
I reach inward to my unfailing spiritual source of dynamic health and life.

I do not reach out in anxiety and fear of life—
I reach inward to God with patience, trust, and love.

I do not reach out for loneliness and in-

security—

I reach inward to that eternal Companion within me, to the indwelling Christ, my constant source of serenity.

Add to this list your own personal denials and affirmations. Make your own list facing this page in your Spiritual Diary by using the following form. Fill in the blank with whatever thought or feeling may be distracting you today from positive spiritual growth.

I do not reach out for _____
I reach inward to the life-giving, peace-giving God within.

Use your own words in this suggested pattern to meet your most immediate needs. You will find that this activity requires honesty and objective thinking. Think what you are directing your thoughts and feelings to right now that is really opposite from the Truth you have learned. Turn away from these particular things; give them no power or attention in your consciousness.

Now go back to the affirmations in section 1 of this Practice Exercise.

I reach inward to the eternal beauty and goodness of the indwelling Christ.

I reach inward to God's infinite wisdom and harmony.

I reach inward to my unfailing spiritual source of dynamic health and life.

I reach inward to God with patience, trust, and love.

I reach inward to that eternal Companion within me, to the indwelling Christ, my constant source of serenity.

Facing this page in your Spiritual Diary, add a page of blank paper on which to write in the affirmations you use in addition to the list above. This list should grow and gain greater significance for you with daily practice.

Repeat each affirmation on both lists; then pause, close your eyes, and as you picture this diagram before you in your mind, think of all your thoughts directed toward the higher self within you; toward God in the midst of you;

toward your own indwelling Christ.

Pause, let your mind feel an inflowing of all your thought power, an inward direction to every sensation and feeling as you use each affirmation. Be sure to follow the pattern of inner reaching, and repeating the statement along with the mental image.

As you practice the exercise each day, you

may find that a particular statement stands out and demands special attention. The affirmation you feel you must emphasize most may vary during the week as you continue to grow and gain spiritual direction and insight.

The still small voice responds to your inward reaching with increasing peace and wisdom. You are learning to contact the spiritual potential within you by aligning your thoughts to your higher self. You begin to experience a calm knowing, an uplifting inspiration, newfound strength and purpose, and an infilling of peace that brings a new dimension to your life.

Here is an idea for consideration in your Spiritual Diary: make a list of whatever *seems* to limit you. Then in the light of what you have learned, think how you may overcome these apparent limitations. Give thanks as you contemplate the ways in which you are now unfolding.

Pattern Three
Lesson 4

Dear Student:

Bless you as you consecrate and dedicate every phase of your life every day by knowing and expressing the Truth that God, the good, is omnipotent and omnipresent.*

*omnipresence—God is everywhere present. There is no place where God is not. He is in all, through all, and around all *(Charles Fillmore, The Revealing Word).*

These ideas have given you a great foundation, a promising beginning. But the spiritual life is not only a process of "beginning," but also always a process of "beginning again." Each time you recognize a Truth, you begin again the process of experiencing and applying it in your own life. All this has to be a part of you, or it is nothing.

You need to begin again now to see yourself—you as an individual, you in every personal and immediate way—in living relationship to the Truth. As a child of God, you have infinite spiritual potential, infinite ability to fulfill the great ideals you envision.

Remember that prayers are with you unceasingly. Great confidence is placed in you as you begin this week's work, for in Truth, you are whole and perfect in spirit, courageous and mighty to do miracles!

PATTERN THREE

Learning to Look Inward

Lesson 4: Oneness

The preceding lessons have provided a basis and an introduction to this final part of Pattern Three. You see how the ideas presented begin to form a related whole. The outline of a practical philosophy has been given; a new way of life emerges. It is not a closed doctrine, but an open and growing philosophy you continually form in your own life around a nucleus of Truth that you can know and experience.

The aim of any religion is defeated if its philosophy seems made up of many disassociated fragments of doctrine. Such a philosophy, however polished, secure, or inspiring it may be, cannot stand the test of life.

If a philosophy is practical, it aids its followers in perceiving life as an integrated whole. It provides a kind of magical equation which, when applied with insight, gives the workable answers to life you seek.

By deduction or induction, the answer is really always the same. Given your own clear evaluation of yourself and your experience, you know that behind and through all things there is something higher, changeless. This you call God. If you begin by induction, assuming first that God is all, you find that everything corroborates this Truth. Or by subtracting from your philosophy all false notions of change and negative appearances, the remaining Truth is the same answer: God is all. Adding all perception, all experience in your mind gives again the same answer: there is a pervading unity and wholeness of existence. All life, all movement, all being is in and of God.

It is not the aim of this lesson to build an intellectual argument, but rather to build a new and uplifting attitude, a feeling of oneness of all things. In the context of pragmatism, there is no profit in seeing life as totally unrelated people and objects. The wisdom and practicality of a philosophy is verified if its purpose is to indicate relationship, sameness, connection, underlying oneness. The use of a teaching is little if it deals only with apparent change, lack, or isolation. But a teaching is never worn out if it reveals that which never changes, lacks nothing, and unifies all things.

Begin again to work this equation in your thinking. Begin with yourself, your own consciousness. If you were to try to express the fact of your consciousness, you would first say, "I am"; then perhaps, "I think," "I feel," "I act," and so on. This "I am" of consciousness you know directly. Indirectly you perceive that same fact of consciousness in others. You sense that this same "stuff" of consciousness is expressed in all people and through all matter in varying ways and degrees.

In reality, you cannot conceive of individual consciousness without being aware of a universal consciousness. Think, too, that this universal body encompasses all matter; this universal mind encompasses all minds.

You must not fight this thought out of fear of losing your "identity." Consider the scriptural truth that you must "lose yourself to find yourself." Only the unreal can ever be lost. Only that which is real can be found. Only the faults, hindrances, or limitations you hold in your consciousness can be lost. Losing these tattered garments of worn-out negative thoughts, you find your real identity as a perfect, beloved child of God, united with Him in all things.

You know that beyond the level of logic, encompassing the countless finite bits and pieces of the universe, is the Infinite. Nothing exists outside of this oneness. This unity embraces all.

When you let your mind rest in the thought of infinite unity, you experience a feeling of wholeness. You begin to know what it is to have a truly "integrated" personality. To integrate is to form into a whole, to bring together in oneness. Your consciousness is integrated when it is brought into harmony with universal consciousness.

In this understanding the loose ends of philosophy are tied. This is the goal of all learning. It is this Truth that all religions point toward, all great individuals perceive. When you are troubled and confused, you are out of contact with this Truth. When you acknowledge it, you are happy and at peace.

The understanding of ultimate unity has mental and physical aspects as well as spiritual aspects. The physical sense of oneness brings to you new strength and wholeness. The body functions with renewed rhythm and balance, for in the transforming activity of Spirit, all cells, organs, and systems work together in harmony. Your physical being becomes a dynamic outpicturing of your consciousness of oneness. All outer facets of your life begin to come together in a pattern of fulfillment. The right place to work and live, the people you need to know and be with, the books you need to read and the things you need to hear, *all* the good you need for a new, unified way of life comes to you surely and in perfect ways as you know and express the Truth. You think thoughts of beauty and goodness and act lovingly and wisely, attracting to you only beautiful experiences. And as you seek the highest, your own highest good comes easily and naturally into your life.

Your mental horizons are boundless when you realize that you are divinely connected to the creative power behind the universe. Know that, in reality, you are in tune with all great thoughts and great thinkers. You are one with infinite wisdom, for the Christ within is the Knower of all things.

The Christ within, Atman, the Over-soul, or God within you is, by whatever term you use, the spiritual faculty of your being. Man has always perceived this spiritual faculty, however vaguely or vividly. In recognizing and expressing this spiritual faculty within him, man is able to manifest his oneness with the infinite mind of God.

He discovers a faculty in himself, and cultivates it until it opens out into a universe of correlated faculties. The farther he goes into mind, the wider its horizon, until he is forced to acknowledge that he is not the personal, limited thing he appears, but the focus of an infinite idea.

That idea contains within itself inexhaustible possibilities. These possibilities are projected into man's consciousness as an image is reflected in a mirror, and, through the powers vested in him, he brings them into manifestation *(Charles Fillmore, Keep a True Lent).*

Stop and consider: you are the "focus of an infinite idea," containing "inexhaustible possibilities." Accept this Truth; let it hold your mind in the thrill of its impact.

As you center your thoughts on this wonderful idea, your immediate experience will be that of a whole cluster of related ideas of great magnitude and force coming quickly to your mind. You begin to feel the powerful meaning of these words as you speak them aloud:

I am the focus of an infinite idea.
I contain inexhaustible possibilities.

You can almost begin to feel the spiritual power within you radiating forth in waves of creative energy. You have discovered what you really are. You have reached inward to accept and focus on God within you, your higher Self. Now you begin to feel the expression of this inner source of love and power welling up within you, ready to be manifested in countless creative ways. There is no limit to your potential, no break in your connection to infinite good. You are one with God, the one Presence and Power in the universe, and you are ready to let that oneness be manifested in your life.

As you bring this sense of oneness into greater manifestation, you find all aspects of your being brought into perfect coordination. Your physical being, as well as your thinking and acting, are brought together in a unity of purpose. This ultimate purpose is full expression of your oneness with God. In this awareness, you know that for every question there is an answer, for every lack there is fulfillment; beneath apparent imperfection, perfection awaits expression.

The recognition of divine connection, of oneness, you developed in Pattern Two is now made more complete. You are one with the universe. You are one with God in and through all creation. And you are one with God within you. Let your physical body manifest that peace, that sense of harmony and wholeness. Let your mind recognize your oneness with the limitless mind of God.

It is this very God Mind within us, which teaches us from within. It is this power which is at work when we feel the need of a better life. . . . It is from this same power that we receive ideas on how to make life better, after the desire to do so has been aroused. Hence, when we say, "Thy will be done on earth as it is in heaven," we are saying we are willing to do our part to make manifest on earth these inner dreams and desires of our own higher self. We are also saying that we quite realize that our own individual mortal minds cannot cope with the problem at hand. We are saying that we are willing and anxious for God to work through us. Which implies, or should imply, our willingness to "wait on the Lord" *(Stella Terrill Mann, Change Your Life through Prayer).*

You may find it helpful to pause after your first reading of this paragraph. Close your eyes and know that the God Mind within you teaches you from within. As you reread the quotation above, realize that through the spiritual authority within you, you are guided in infinite love and wisdom.

Know that right now, you are receiving the answers you need, the inspiration and the insight you need to live in conscious oneness with God. Beyond physical striving and mental searching, that oneness is eternal Truth. In "waiting on the Lord," you let go of all inner resistance to the manifestation of perfect unity with God. Before you go on with your practice exercise, wait a moment. Register in your mind the feeling of pausing to listen within. Quietly know that you are one with God, the good omnipotent, and all things are possible.

Practice Exercise

Read through each section of the exercise, then put aside your papers and practice it. At the end of each session, be sure to make notes of your thoughts and experiences in your Spiritual Diary.

Step 1. Begin by sitting in your chair with spine straight, both feet on the floor. Let your hands rest, palms open, in your lap. Release all tension from your body. As you feel the tightness leave your muscles, let all anxiety leave your thoughts. Know that all misconceptions about your true self—all thoughts of weakness or limitation—are now released and let go. You can see yourself in your mind as perfect and pure. You are changeless, immutable, eternal, free spirit. Rest in this thought as you say the words:

I am eternal, free Spirit.

A feeling of wholeness overcomes all conflict in your mind and body. As eternal, free Spirit, you know that you are one with God. Repeat the affirmation to yourself silently, resting completely in the peace of this oneness.

Step 2. See in your mind the cone image you used in the exercise in Pattern Three, Lesson 2. See it revolve in your mind so that you may look inward, to its apex. All of your thoughts are moving inward. Feel that your attention is turning away from any outer condition in life, ever inward, deeper and deeper, to that source of perfect peace and oneness within you. You can see the light of your spiritual self shining there at the point of the cone, shining within you as the reference point, the point of unity of all things. Here all things are brought together. Here is your point of guidance, your source of unending strength, your ultimate focus of all love, all wisdom. If your thoughts should begin to turn away from your inward center, visualize once more the cone image, and remind yourself of your purpose with these words:

I turn inward to God within me.

Step 3. With your attention turned to God within you, use your will to bring all your thought-energy into direct communion with that inner self. Think of the diagram of the

arrows directed toward a central point.

Think that you are actively reaching within you right now for the still small voice of spiritual understanding. Affirm:

I do not reach outward to negative appearances,

I reach inward to the life-giving, peace-giving Christ within.

Think of this inner reaching activity. Give it the whole force of your mind and heart. As you reach inward with your whole being, you begin to sense a point of contact. You touch the changeless spiritual center within you. You subtract the unreal, leaving the real in your thoughts; you turn away from the finite to the infinite; you turn from duality to oneness.

This activity of reaching inward is like an "inbreathing" of Spirit to the one focal point of your inner self. Repeat the affirmation:

I reach inward to the life-giving, peace-giving Christ within.

Step 4. Immediately your mind comes to a quiet meeting place of Spirit as you stand in oneness with God. Now is the time of "waiting" as you rest here in patient stillness. Know that you dwell in spiritual peace and wholeness. You begin to experience an "out-breathing" of Spirit through you. This requires no effort, no forcing of thought energy, no activity of will. It is the natural expression of the Christ within, the natural outflow of God's love. The light of God shines forth from within you into every part of your being, just as this diagram indicates.

As you remain poised in this experience,

you can feel this spiritual energy flowing through you to unify every phase of your life. In thankfulness and praise, carry this experience of true spiritual oneness with you as you close your study time. During the week, think again of the process of recognizing your true self, turning within, reaching inward, and waiting while the loving activity of God within breathes out through you to bring into unity all facets of existence. In your Spiritual Diary describe this process in your own words, according to your own experience. And always give thanks as you think of the ways in which you are ever unfolding! Know the truth of these affirmations as you speak them aloud and then silently as you rest in the peace of this spiritual experience:

I am at one with God.

God is all—I know and express oneness with God.

There comes a time in this activity when the final affirmation is a silent knowing, a wordless realization that God is all. In this realization, your life becomes an expression of spiritual oneness; you find true happiness and peace.

Pattern Four

Lesson 1

Dear Student:

You know that the Truth you are learning is not merely an arrangement of words, but that these words suggest great ideas, and ideas signal results. In the space of every day, you experience that undeniable tendency of ideas to suggest action!

A great idea can come to you with the momentum of a great inhalation of air. An idea can be like a dynamic intake of new vitality. Instantaneously with such an experience, you feel ready to breathe out into your life the fullness of your thought!

PATTERN FOUR

Learning Wholeness

Lesson 1: Believing

As you continue to keep a time and place reserved for this study, and as you assume a poised physical and mental attitude in your exercises, you are establishing a spiritual atmosphere of thinking and living. Through this discipline, you become increasingly open and receptive to the Christ within you. As you openly and freely receive the wisdom of the Christ within, you express peace, goodness, and happiness openly and freely.

In your attitudes and in the words you speak, in your thoughts and in your actions, you express the Truth you are learning more freely and perfectly every day. As you grow in awareness, the presence of God within you shines forth like a great light illuminating and lifting your attitudes, your physical being, and all the people and conditions of your life.

Think of the wonderful results you have already experienced! In every way you feel more alive and happier than ever before. You feel more in tune and at one with the universe

185

than you have ever felt before.

You know that this spiritual oneness is your constant, normal condition. It is a growing sense of harmony, peace, and wholeness that can never really be taken away. Any thought or experience that does not fully manifest this ultimate Truth is only a partial reality. As you lift your thinking to a consciousness of the Christ within, perfect wholeness is manifest throughout all phases of your life. In your relationships and attitudes as well as in your physical body, you experience health* as never before.

*health—a state of being sound or whole in mind and body. Oneness with the Christ Mind assures perfect health. Health is the normal condition of man, a condition true to the Truth of his being *(Charles Fillmore, The Revealing Word)*.

You are a many-faceted being, of countless moods and phases of expression. Yet there is within you an element of the nonrelative, the changeless, the Christ within. When you open your mind to the great idea of your oneness with the Christ, this idea is inevitably expressed in your life.

You have hit upon the concept of perfection. Already you perceive that the strength of that idea is unlimited. As surely as you can conceive of God as ultimate good, and as surely as you believe that this good can be known and manifested, you receive and express unlimited good.

If you believe that God is immanent in the material world, and if you believe that He is now within you, existing constantly as perfect good expressing in and through you and the universe, then you are ready to believe that perfect healing in outer conditions and in your own body and mind is a reality that can be experienced.

Charles Fillmore wrote, "The first step in all spiritual healing is to believe . . . " *(The Revealing Word).* Take this step now with all your mind and heart. Hold to this wonderful ability to believe; it is the tendency of your mind toward the highest Truth.

Believe that healing in every part of your life is a dynamic and reachable experience that can come through many channels. Believe that mental healing can come about for you through counseling or individual study and unfoldment. Believe that healing activity in your affairs can come about through right

187

decisions and a patient and loving attitude. Believe that physical healing can come about through doctors and medication, and through balanced living. But beyond all these ways of healing, know that true healing always begins with a thrill of recognition in your innermost self; it is above all else a *spiritual awakening* that is real, deep, transforming, and lasting.

You can find many illustrations of this kind of awakening in the New Testament, where the healings of Jesus are described.* Find such a description in the Bible and read it slowly and thoughtfully so that you may more clearly understand the spiritual process of healing. This is the process you seek to experience in your own mind and affairs as well as in your physical being.

In many passages of the Bible, Jesus asked individuals if they believed they could be healed. As you read these verses, is there not something within you that answers, "I believe"; is there not something within you that is receptive to perfection, ready to be healed?

*(See, for example, one or more of the following: Matthew 9:27-30; Mark 5:35-42; Mark 9:14-29; John 5:2-9; John 11:17-44.)

Read this part of the story once again, and try really to feel the impact of the words. Imagine that you are the person in the story who is in need of healing, and feel that Jesus is speaking directly to you. You can hear His voice in your mind, and you can feel your whole being responding in readiness to be blessed. You begin to release any trace of doubt or fear as you hold in your mind the idea of perfect, immediate healing. Now register the feeling.

———

You respond to the words of Jesus because there is that in you which is of the same divine authority as Jesus Christ. To that inner self, all things are possible. Listen now with your mind and heart to that still, small voice saying: "Believe and be healed. Believe and be healed."

Your thinking is immediately lifted and harmonized by the words, and your body responds in a feeling of wholeness. You know that every activity of your life is now blessed and unified. Rest in the certainty of the healing power and love of the Christ.

———

The Christ that is within you is all-wise,

all-powerful, all-loving, perfect. When your mind is centered on the Christ within, you cannot at the same time hold thoughts of limitation, for it is the nature of your Christ self to change whatever is negative to positive, to banish confusion and restore harmony, to transform imperfection to perfection, to bring perfect wholeness and health.

Consider carefully the definition of *health* that has been given in this part of Pattern Four. To be "whole" is to be conscious of oneness with God, the one Presence and Power in the universe. This experience starts in your own mind as you begin to believe. Believe that God *is* the one Presence and Power, and that oneness with God can *now* be realized and manifested in your life as wholeness in body, mind, and affairs.

Hold in mind whatever condition of your life may be in need of healing. Carry this need to the Christ within; lift your needs in faith and love to that high point of Spirit within you. Here all need is answered, all is made perfect and whole.

If you are in need of mental healing, remember that beneath the changing moods of your mind exists your inner Christ self; this true self is ever free of all limits. It is all-wise, all-powerful, and all-loving. It cannot hold a grudge or be afraid; it cannot ever be foolish or unkind. It is free of all that is negative or restricting, and expresses only perfect wisdom, love, strength, and wholeness. Believe in the infinite Spirit within you, and know that you cannot be enslaved by any thought or memory. Healing in your thoughts and feelings can take place at this moment to free you from any anxiety you may be experiencing. Believe in the freeing Truth that God is powerful to heal and harmonize your thoughts. You will discover that seeing all things in the light of Truth transmutes regrets and confining thoughts to life-giving, inspired ideas. You will discover that apparent limits to your understanding and happiness are dissolved as your mind turns to the activity of believing in God's infinite power and love.

If you are in need of physical healing, believe that there is within you an unchanging source of limitless strength and beauty. Right now, you are whole and perfect in Spirit, and as you begin consciously to know this Truth, physical vitality and balance begin to manifest in you. As you believe in the reality of the loving and dynamic presence of God within you, mighty to heal and bless, good health is reflected in your physical being.

If the conditions of your life are in a confused state and if people around you or you yourself seem to be making wrong decisions or seem to be caught in unhappy, unproductive situations, you can begin now to release the sense of bondage and conflict in your own mind. You know that in reality, you are eternal, free Spirit. Nothing can keep you from realizing and expressing your true, spiritual nature. As you hold to this center of balance and wisdom within you, the wholeness and harmony you seek begins to show forth in your life and in the lives of all with whom you come in contact. Believing in the healing power of God becomes a constructive and fulfilling way of life; a way that is based on Truth.

You do not really need to be "convinced" about Truth. This is not a subject to be argued about, for it stands outside of argument. Truth is not a thing that you can be made to believe; rather, it is like something that you already know, and have forgotten that you know. Believing in Truth is a kind of

192

recognition of what has always been true. Concurrent with this conscious recognition is the expression through you of the unity, harmony, and wholeness that is characteristic of Truth.

You believe in the alternation of day and night; you believe in the cycle of seasons; you believe in the things you see and touch every day; you believe in your own life and identity. Yet you have touched with your mind the changeless Truth beyond and within all things. You sense that beyond the alternation of day and night, beside the cycle of the seasons, and within the things of everyday exists the omnipresent, omnipotent, omniscient Being whose very nature is perfection, peace, love. You believe in your own name, age, situation, experience, yet you cannot help but believe that you are more than you appear to be. And you perceive that all persons are more than they appear to be.

You begin to believe that in spite of the confusion and conflict you see in the world, peace is not a mere abstraction, but a latent reality. Although there is poverty and ignorance in the world, you begin to believe that infinite supply and infinite wisdom are everywhere available to all at this moment. You see evidence of antagonism and sickness, yet you see a higher, truer evidence of an all-pervading, unifying, and life-giving divine love.

Believe in this higher evidence! Let the recognition of God as the divine, omnipresent, all-powerful Healer be expressed through you in new wholeness in your body, mind, and affairs. By believing in the Truth, you open the way to experience infinite blessings.

Practice Exercise

. Still your body and open your mind to receive only the highest Truth. Let your thoughts come away from outer things and dwell only on God within you as you affirm aloud:

There is but one Presence and one Power in the universe—God, the good omnipotent.

Take time to believe and to understand as you repeat this affirmation several times with your eyes closed.

The statement may be used in the sense of a denial when you emphasize the words, "but *one* Presence and *one* Power." Know that there is no outside destructive force in the world, only a limited perception of God, who is ultimate good, everywhere present, and all-powerful. As you open your mind and heart in an attitude of sincere believing, you become receptive to higher and greater understanding of the inherent wholeness of all things.

Do not let distracting thoughts interfere with your spiritual progress. The more intensely you can dwell on this simple exercise and the less you turn away in your mind toward outer things, the deeper will be your understanding, and the greater your joy today and in the days that follow. There is no idea more true or transforming than that God is the one Presence, the one Power. Therefore, let go of all other thoughts and direct your mind only to this dynamic idea as you speak these words:

There is but one Presence and one Power in my mind—God, the good omnipotent.

Hold the thought. Fear, resentment, envy, anger, or distrust cannot disturb you, for your mind is filled with the presence of God. Imagine that this presence is like a great light illuminating your head. Close your eyes now and hold this image.

You are experiencing mental healing and cleansing. If at any time you feel almost "overtaken" by some unwanted attitude, think of the light of God's presence filling your mind. You feel lifted and illumined by this activity, for you begin to know for yourself:

God is the one Presence and Power in my mind.

Believe the Truth of this statement and rest in it wholly, as you say the words silently.

Think now of your physical self; believe and affirm this affirmation first aloud and then silently and slowly:

There is but one Presence and one Power in my body—God, the good omnipotent.

You know that there is no destructive force in your body, working to tear down or create imbalance, for in reality, all is in perfect harmony, in tune with the Infinite, at one with God. God within you is mighty to heal and strengthen, powerful to rebuild and replenish. No apparent weakness or disorder can resist the healing power of God, once you set this power into motion by believing. Sit very still for several moments, and consciously receive the activity of healing into every cell of your body.

Close your eyes and imagine your whole body filled with healing light as you rest in the certainty:

God is the one Presence and Power in my body.

If you find that some situation confronting you in life comes often to your mind during your study period, consciously bless the situation—bring it into a spiritual context. As you think of this situation, speak this affirmation of the Truth you believe:

There is but one Presence and one Power in my affairs—God, the good omnipotent.

You are now involved in the work of knowing and living the highest Truth. It is an ever-expanding activity, a constant challenge. Therefore, speak the words of the statement with firmness and intensity.

Then speak the words once more, this time softly in peaceful acceptance. You do not need to be convinced, for you know that the words are true.

Hold a picture in your mind of those around you in your family, of individuals you work with and deal with, or perhaps of individuals who may be far away, yet are close in your thoughts. See these individuals filled with the light of God's presence. Know that with each of them resides the presence and power of God. God is now expressed through them as patience and peace, as understanding and right judgment, and as love and perfect wholeness. Believe and accept with thanksgiving the reality that in your life and in the lives of those you are thinking about today,
God is the one Presence and Power.

Close your eyes as you speak the words again softly and peacefully,
God is the one Presence and Power.

Believing has opened the way for receiving. You receive the healing activity of God into every part of your life, and you are lifted and illumined by this realization of Truth. As you realize Truth, it is "made real" in and through

198

you. Give thanks that this *is so.*

Take time now, as you close your study period, to write in your Spiritual Diary of the new wholeness you are experiencing in your thinking and feeling, in your physical being, and in your relationships with others. As you practice this exercise during the week, it may be helpful to write down the affirmations in the order in which they appear, to work with each one once more, and then to record your own insights about the healing process. Always consider the ways in which you are now unfolding.

As you proceed in your study, continually give thanks for the growing recognition that God, the good omnipotent, is the one Presence and Power in the universe. Give thanks for the happiness and wholeness that are now being made manifest in your life.

Pattern Four
Lesson 2

Dear Student:

Remember how you felt when reading and thinking about some part of the preceding lesson material that had special and deeply stimulating meaning for you. Remember the mental sensation of intake, and the immediate impulse to give forth what you had discovered.

If this experience can be described, it is like being suddenly uplifted, it is like a tremendous overcoming, it is like a total release, yet it is also like receiving a priceless gift; it is inexpressible joy. With this joy comes an overwhelming sense of fulfillment, of oneness.

This feeling that you are "brimming" with an idea is the sign of true spiritual development. You are experiencing the excitement of spiritual fullness and the irresistible impulse to express the Truth!

PATTERN FOUR

Learning Wholeness

Lesson 2: Choosing

Through daily exercise and thought, you have come to believe the wonderful truth that you can be healed of every limitation, that you can be renewed, cleansed, and made whole in every way. By believing, you are following your spiritual inclination toward infinite wisdom and infinite good. And as you reach out with all your being toward a fuller realization of wholeness, you begin to let go of any thoughts and conditions that do not reflect this ideal.

You can no longer accept any pain, any anxiety, any lack as the best that life has to offer, for you know that life offers you perfect wholeness. Anything less than perfect wholeness is only a part of life. Once you have accepted the challenge of seeking true happiness and fulfillment, you cannot settle for less. Ask your inner self, "Can I be healed of any imperfection?" You know from the truth you have learned and experienced that there is no true reason why you cannot be made perfectly whole. The answer comes, "I can be made whole in every perfect way." Through believing, through right choice and active faith, "I can" becomes "I am."

The process of healing begins when your mind is made ready for healing. You begin with "I believe"; you work with your thinking and feeling so that you reach "I know"; and then the process begins to manifest as "I am." You believe in healing, in perfection, as your natural state. You are working with ideas so that you can begin to know the real truth about yourself. This truth is becoming a part of your thinking and feeling. As wholeness becomes a reality in your life, you know and manifest the Truth: "I am whole."

You know that you are not reaching toward a mere "dream" of health or a shaky possibility of true wholeness and well-being. You are reaching toward a dynamic *reality*, an actual state of existence that you can bring into your awareness and that can be made manifest in your life. You are reaching toward an ideal.

Charles Fillmore defined *ideal* as "a mental pattern of perfection" *(The Revealing Word).* You can realize and manifest an ideal—you can hold a mental pattern of perfection—because back of all the changing conditions of your life, back of all the appearances about you, back of all the countless impressions of your mind lies the absolute perfection of Spirit. By believing with love and expectation, you are making ready for the *realization* of this ideal.

You know that realizing an ideal involves a great challenge. Strength and discipline as well as faith and love are needed. Ideals of equality, freedom, honor, achievement, beauty, goodness, purity, and peace have held the imagination and inspired the activities of mankind throughout all time. Yet no ideal is more challenging, heroic, or inspiring than the ideal of absolute wholeness for which you are reaching now.

Take a moment now to close your eyes and let the thought of perfect wholeness inspire you. Imagine yourself completely whole and perfect physically, mentally, and in all your affairs. See yourself strong and ready right now to do great things!

This is truly a heroic idea. As you hold to this idea, instantly you sit up straighter and you tend to look at things in a more lofty and courageous way. You *are* ready to know and do great things!

But if you should think instead that you are weak and ill and that there is no escape from suffering and troubles, you would begin to feel your shoulders slump. Any little discomfort you might feel would become intensified; any problem you might hold in your mind would seem unsolvable. It is almost impossible to imagine yourself doing any great thing when you think in a small, negative way.

But no limited thought can really hold you, once you have been inspired by your ideal of perfection. Remember that when you began this course, something within you urged you to try a new way of thinking, a new way of life. The Spirit within you is ever strong, ever steadfast and heroic, and is never satisfied with half-truths or with partial manifestation of wholeness. It does not accept the finality of any negative appearance, for it is ever choosing that which is ultimately true.

Imagine that you have two pictures of yourself. In one, you are frowning, and you appear weak and ill. In the other, you are smiling, and you look strong and radiant. In choosing which picture to keep and enjoy, you would naturally choose the one that emphasizes your best traits. As you look at this picture, you think, "I choose this one, because it looks most like me; it shows me as I really am."

In all things, it is natural for you to choose beauty, joy, and wholeness, for in reality, you are eternal, free Spirit. Consciously or unconsciously you know that it is your very nature to be healthy, happy, and successful, and you respond in inner and outer ways to that which suggests your true nature. You respond to ideas of wholeness naturally, easily, and consistently as you learn to let go of restricting habits of thought. In this way, you clear the way for the inspiration of Truth, and you make ready to experience positive results. According to your inner guidance, reaffirm your choice for a higher, better way of thinking and living. Choose again to fulfill your spiritual destiny.

In all growth and development, the factor of choice is inescapable. There is no way that a living philosophy can be imparted to you unless *you choose* to live it yourself. Living involves constant choice; you must decide every day of your life what to do, where to go, or what to buy, and you must make thousands of other great and small decisions about yourself and your life. But if you analyze each of these decisions carefully, you begin to see that all of the choices you make in the space of a day are really based on one reference point only, and that is the decision, "How shall I think?"

Consider whether in your thoughts and words you are following your natural, spiritual inclination to choose for yourself what you really are. The ideas you hold about yourself and your life are not separate from your experience, but are the central shaping force and direction of your life.

Analyze the kinds of thoughts you have. Thoughts can be heavy burdens of negation, false impressions, or limited judgments that you must carry with you everywhere like very heavy stones. These thoughts are troublesome and uncomfortable; they bring down the level of your expectations and limit the good you experience. Yet thoughts may also be positive, lifted, inspired; these thoughts are like beautiful flowers that you carry through life lightly, easily, and joyously. They ever increase and brighten your expectations, and they open the way for unlimited good in your life.

By the thoughts you think, do you constantly choose the positive, harmonizing, healing activity of God for yourself and for others? Remember that all things begin with ideas. If your own ideas are happy, positive, constructive ideas, the results in your attitudes, in your body, and in your affairs will be happy, positive, and constructive results. But if your thoughts are sad, negative, and destructive, only like results can come about for you.

It is important for you to think about what you want your life to be like, for by the thoughts you think, you constantly color and form your world. By your own choice, life can be drudgery for you, or it can be beautiful and happy. If you are in need of healing, if you are confused in your mind or in your affairs, you must begin now to hold a mental pattern of perfection. Hold to the ideal of wholeness.

Sift your thoughts; weigh the words you speak. Choose only positive ideas among the words you hear and read. Do not let false, negative perceptions about yourself or about others from *any* source be accepted into your thinking. Quietly and firmly, in an inward way, deny limitation and affirm infinite good. Choose for yourself what you will think and what you will not think. Admit into your consciousness only that which you know to be true.

✓The use of denial and affirmation in positive thinking is not a turning away from reality; it is rather the activity of seeing beyond false appearances to a higher, truer perception of reality. You may say to yourself, "But if my house is falling down around me, it will not help me to shut my eyes and refuse to look at what is happening." True, if you should think only, "My house is falling! My house is falling!" then certainly you would be helpless. In such a case you must recognize the need for constructive action, and you must begin this action by picturing the house beautifully rebuilt. You need to hold a mental pattern of perfection. Then, according to this perfect plan, the rebuilding begins. All outer steps you may take toward rebuilding the house—whether you ask an architect to help you plan or hire a carpenter to help you build—begin with your own inner decision not to dwell on the negative appearances, but to realize the *ideal.*

By positive, enlightened thinking, you are able to bring your ideal into manifestation. You can release into your life the unlimited healing, unifying power contained within you. Think wholeness, health, balance, and these ideas are manifested in your body as physical strength, energy, and vitality. Think wisdom, creativity, happiness, and these ideas are manifested in your mind as clear understanding, constructive activity, and joy and tranquillity. Think prosperity, love, harmony, and these ideas are manifested in your affairs as abundant supply, cooperative interactions with others, and peace. Build the awareness that with every thought you think, you are making the choice for wholeness or separation, and at this moment you are choosing the kind of life you live.

Ask yourself the question now: "What kind

of life will I have?" Know that you can *will* to be happy and whole. You have the power to direct your will away from negative thoughts and toward positive results.

As you reach toward positive results, you must release your mental hold on all that is false or limiting. Reaching toward your ideal of wholeness, you must give up utterly any thought that God wills sickness or unhappiness for you.

√ God's will has nothing at all to do with the need for healing that we may have, no matter what that need is. The only part God's will plays is to help us get well. His will for us is always good; it could be nothing else, for He is good. He sees only good for us, He has only good prepared for us. This good must include health of body, mind, emotions, finances, relationships, anything and everything that has to do with us and our personal affairs *(Mary Katherine MacDougall, Healing Now).*

You must also give up completely any thought that wholeness and health in every area of life is in any way unnatural or that it is too much to hope for.

210

The more enlightened man becomes, the greater is his desire for perfect health. This is logical, for to be healthy is natural *(Charles Fillmore, Jesus Christ Heals).*

Health is the normal condition of man and of all creation. We find that there is an omnipresent principle of health pervading all living things. Health, real health, is from within and does not have to be manufactured in the without. Health is the very essence of Being. It is as universal and enduring as God *(Charles Fillmore, Jesus Christ Heals).*

There is that within you that stands apart from the endless stream of your thoughts. Centered in that Christ self, you learn to watch your thinking and to guide and control your mind. More and more, you begin to reject heavy, unhappy thinking, and to choose instead a way of thinking that is light and happy. As you exercise your spiritual ability to direct the trend of your thoughts in a positive way, the blessings of wholeness you begin to experience in all facets of your life are without end.

All things begin to fit together in a pattern

of inner and outer harmony and perfection. You begin to experience true healing. Healing may be experienced in the harmony of body tissues and organs. Healing may be experienced in logical, clear thinking, in love and understanding. Habits that once bound and restricted your thinking are loosed; answers come to questions that once seemed unanswerable; attitudes and feelings begin to turn from fear and resentment to acceptance and forgiveness. Other people and conditions around you begin to reflect the spiritual unity you are experiencing and demonstrating. You actively choose spiritual wholeness, and through the infinite power of God within you, you are made wonderfully whole!

Practice Exercise

As you settle yourself in your study place today, begin to direct the power of your mind constructively and lovingly. Think about yourself and your life. As you watch your thoughts, do not mentally "claim" an illness; don't think of it as "my ailment," "my bad knee," "my cold." These negative conditions cannot possibly belong to that pure self of you. If you have decided to choose vitality and wholeness over pain and imbalance, then in thought and word let go of your claim to sickness, vulnerability, and disease, and hold to the ideal of perfect health. Repeat this statement firmly to yourself, aloud and then silently:

I deny negative conditions in my body, and I hold to the positive ideal of wholeness.

Breathe in health! Feel wholeness in every part of your body. Nothing is held back; you choose sickness for no part of you. You choose only health.

Give thanks that right now, the healing, harmonizing power of God is active in your body. Through this power, you are made whole.

Do not claim a disturbed state of mind. Never say aloud or to yourself: "I am a neurotic," "I am foolish," or "I am sinful." Remember that your true self is in perfect balance and is infinitely wise and pure. If you have decided that you want peace of mind and divine guidance, then release your claim to anger, ignorance, and depression, and hold instead in thought and word to the ideal of perfect mental wholeness. Repeat this statement firmly to yourself, aloud and then silently:

I deny negative attitudes in my mind, and I hold to the positive ideal of wholeness.

Breathe in peace of mind. Feel wholeness filling your thoughts. Nothing is held back; you choose no negative thought or feeling. You choose only love and joy.

Give thanks that at this very moment, the healing, harmonizing power of God is active in your mind, and you are whole and happy.

Do not claim for yourself or for others any limiting outer conditions. Don't say silently or aloud: "We'll never have the money and comfort we need," "Things will never work out right," or "There can never be peace." You do not believe these negative statements, for you know that within all people and in and through all situations exists God, the good omnipotent. If you have decided to align yourself and your life with infinite goodness, abundance, and peace, then let negation fall away from your thinking and remove it from your speech. Seek in every place and in all people only the goodness of God. Repeat this statement firmly to yourself, aloud and then silently:

I deny all that seems negative in my life

*and in the lives of others, and I hold to the
positive ideal of wholeness.*

Breathe in harmony. Feel wholeness filling
your affairs and spreading throughout the
world. Nothing is held back; you choose no
negative condition. You choose only peace
and the highest good for all.

Give thanks with all your mind and heart
that the healing, harmonizing power of God is
now active in your life and in the lives of all
others to bring understanding, prosperity,
peace, and unity.

As you go forth each day, watch your
thoughts and the thoughts to which you give
force in words. Think to yourself often, "In
what ways am I now unfolding?" Write in
your Spiritual Diary your own denials and
affirmations to meet your specific needs for
wholeness. And as you use these statements
and practice this exercise, constantly hold
before you your highest idea. Continually give
thanks that through the loving, strengthening
guidance of God within you, you are now
realizing this ideal!

Pattern Four

Lesson 3

Dear Student:

You have come into a sense of oneness through a kind of circular pattern of unfoldment. The first step is an attitude of receptivity; then as you recognize and accept an idea as Truth, and as you begin to express this new awareness in your life, your sense of wholeness and unity leads you to understand that Truth is inherently whole and unifying.

Every understanding you reach suggests other Truth ideas, and you continually grow to become ever more open to God in mind and heart, to receive great ideas, and to know and express freely the blessings you experience. This cycle of receiving and expressing is characteristic of all spiritual growth. Within this pattern of unfoldment lie the infinite possibilities of seeking and finding God.

The wonderful idea that you can find God, that you are in reality at one with God, is the idea that underlies all Truth. When you realize this great idea, when you feel your mind "brimming" with this thought, the expression of this realization in your life is certain!

PATTERN FOUR

Learning Wholeness

Lesson 3: Balance

In your thoughts and words, you are seeking to see things in right perspective and to express a higher perception about life. As you become attuned to God, all phases of your life reach a "spiritual balance."

Inherent in the idea of spiritual balance is the thought process of mentally "weighing" your attitudes and concepts. In this process you develop spiritual discrimination. "What shall I hold, what shall I let go; what is true, what is untrue?" is the continual mood of your thought. As you think in this way, you begin to reach a higher level of understanding and equanimity. You begin to experience more fully the impact of your ideal.

The ideal of wholeness implies practice, which means concentrated effort and self-discipline. There are no magic words that will bring it, for it is a total condition of mind and body. However, as you let words suggest to you powerful ideas of positive Truth, the effect on your life may seem "magical"; in reality, the blessings of spiritual practice in your life are the natural outpicturing of the divine ideas you are realizing.

You are discovering that as you become receptive to healing, as you begin to believe and to choose for yourself right understanding about wholeness, the spiritual process of healing comes peacefully and easily in a quiet, inner way. Beyond the mental discipline, even beyond the affirmation of Truth, divine healing in mind, body, and affairs is an innate and natural tendency.

You find that after focusing all your attention on particular healing needs for a time, after struggling to deny negative thought patterns and working to affirm positive ideas, you reach a point of great release. Your mind will no longer hold to the problem you have been working with; instead, it begins to center more and more on God. At first, you recognize a need for healing; you think of the need itself. Then you affirm that God heals this need. You begin to realize that wholeness is the divine reality. Your mind centers in the thought of wholeness. When you have reached this point in experience, you may begin by thinking, "I have a need for wholeness in a certain area of my life." Then you affirm, "God is all-powerful to heal me." At this point you begin to realize, "In my mind, body, and affairs, God is the one presence and power . . . God is." In this way you experience the inclination to focus away from a particular finite need and to be drawn more and more to thoughts of the Infinite. Your mind will tend to move away from concentration on one particular area of your life, and will begin to gravitate to the spiritual center of your life, God within you. When you feel this inner tendency, your healing has truly begun. This is the transition from disorder to order, from need to wholeness, from imbalance to balance. You see a part of reality, then more and more you perceive the whole.

You perceive that there is no more or less

of God now than there ever was—that there is no scarcity of perfection, no lack of good, no unsolvable problem, no incurable health need. Every atom of the universe is complete and perfect *now*. All beauty is inherent in every particle of the world, just as God is inherent in every particle of the world. All energy, capacity, and wholeness await expression at this moment; God awaits expression at this moment. Right now, all good is everywhere present and reachable; God is everywhere present and reachable. All need is already fulfilled; all is already in divine order and perfect balance. You need only recognize it. Think of this truth!

Use whatever analogy is comfortable to you in order to experience it: think that the realization of spiritual wholeness and balance is like opening a door; it is like switching on an electric current, tuning into a higher frequency, deeply inhaling pure, fresh air; it is like stepping into the sunlight. Write down your own idea about the experience in your Spiritual Diary and use it over and over again as a way to direct your thoughts and heighten your perception of wholeness and balance. Think of this experience—feel it happening to you.

Whatever way you like to think of the experience of being perfectly whole, perfectly in balance with God, know that it is real and immediate. When you receive medical help, know that it is signaling the natural balance and wholeness in your body. If you rearrange outer conditions in your life, know that you are allowing the natural divine order of things to prevail. If you are gaining insight and peace of mind from your work in this course, know that this is because something within you is already perfectly peaceful, balanced, and all-wise, and you are now *realizing* it.

> You need to think of God, the all-powerful Healer, as being already within you, in every part of your mind, heart, and body. . . .
>
> Sometimes we pray to a God outside of ourselves. It is the God in the midst of us that frees and heals *(Myrtle Fillmore's Healing Letters).*

Contemplate the words, "God is the *all-powerful* Healer." The infinite power of God within you transcends all physical limits. Through Him all things are possible. Earnestly know for yourself:

God, the all-powerful Healer, is now in the midst of me.

Rest in that thought—think of God as the active healing, balancing force throughout your body, your mind, and in all of your life.

As you attune your mind to God, you free the unlimited healing power within you. As you center in the thought of God, thoughts of limitation or negative appearances begin to fall away from you. You begin to experience God as present and active in and through you.

With our eye of faith we must see God in our flesh, see that wholeness for which we are praying in every part of the body temple. "Know ye not that your body is a temple of the Holy Spirit which is in you . . . glorify God therefore in your body" *(Myrtle Fillmore's Healing Letters).*

Your body is the temple of God; in every cell is housed the divine life force, seeking expression in the activity of every organ and tissue. Seeing your body as the temple of God helps you to hold it in love and respect. As you realize that your body is precious and blessed, that it is a "sacred house," you are especially careful to live with a consciousness of balance.

As you see your mind as the divine channel for God's infinite wisdom and understanding, you become increasingly aware of the need to keep balance in your emotions and to keep attuned to divine ideas. You know that anger and fear are destructive, because they bring a sense of isolation and distress that directly affects your physical being and brings confusion into your life. As you become a clear channel for God's love and understanding, you keep your thoughts centered on Him and your mind is inspired and tranquil.

You know that any action that is destructive or negative causes an imbalance in your life. Therefore, you express the ideal of wholeness and spiritual balance in all things. You act lovingly and creatively, and your life is in divine order.

As you think about yourself, as you consider your mind, body, and all the affairs of your life, bless each phase of your being; confer good upon your life. As you think of your physical body, think of it as the temple of God, loved, blessed, sanctified, and whole. As you think of your mind, think of it as the

223

perfect channel for God's expression; it is inspired, happy, positive, creative, and whole. As you think of your affairs, confer good upon every area of your activity. See your relationship with your family, your business associates, your friends, and with *all* mankind as harmonized, blessed, and unified by divine love. Realize that God is now present and active in all things, in all people. He is all-powerful, all-loving, all-knowing, One. God is perfect balance, perfect wholeness. Give thanks as you hold this thought:

God is perfect balance, perfect wholeness.

If ever you think you may be reacting to pressures of conditions around you so that you fear you may become ill or disturbed, or that you might somehow fail in your endeavors, restore balance by turning inward and resting in the knowledge that God is the all-powerful Healer of all conditions, inner and outer. *God is perfect balance and wholeness.*

Affirm the good in your life and in your affairs—see God in all things. Nothing can weaken or harm you, nothing can upset you, if you hold firmly to the idea of spiritual balance and oneness with God. You can meet any responsibility with poise and confidence, without succumbing to illness or losing your peace of mind, for you live in the certainty that divine order and wholeness are manifesting in your life, and that all things are in balance with God.

You have no need that cannot be filled. You have no pain that cannot be healed. You have no emptiness or lack that cannot be answered. You need only recognize that God is infinite fulfillment, infinite abundance, infinite health and happiness. Open your mind to the unlimited possibilities of good that are prepared for you, and know that truly all things are possible through God, the good omnipotent.

In spite of the apparently endless frailties of the human psychophysical makeup, God within you is ever lifting you to health, ever seeking to express ideas of perfection and eternity through you. You have only to recognize this freeing truth. Already you feel an increasing tendency toward perfection that you cannot resist. More and more, you draw on your inner source of goodness and beauty. More and more your mind becomes receptive to God's quickening life.

To be continuously healthy we must draw on the one and only source of life, God. God is Spirit, and Spirit pours its quickening life into mind and body when we turn our attention to it and make ourself receptive by trusting Spirit to restore us to harmony and health *(Charles Fillmore, Jesus Christ Heals).*

Back of every moment's activity of your life and within every cell of your body and through every molecule of the material world, God exists as the one Presence and the one Power in the universe. This is the reality you are growing to believe and understand; this is the Truth behind all truths:

God is the one Presence and Power in the universe.

There is no place in your body where the power of God does not reside. Feel your pulse; what power, what life can this be, but God's power, God's life? Listen to the regular, rhythmic sound of your own breathing. You can perceive that there is within you a ceaseless, tireless life force, constantly working to build and replenish your physical body. The wonder of wonders is that a scratch on your arm naturally mends, and heals; that the bread you eat is transformed into living tissue and energy; that life-giving oxygen is derived from the air you breathe; that you are able to sleep and rest, and then awaken to rise and walk; that you sit here now, reading and assimilating these ideas, ready to go forth and *live* them.

You who look for a miracle, find a mirror—look around you! This life you are living right now, with all its energy and possibility, is the greatest miracle of all time!

Think of the wonderful power of your mind. In a microsecond, a thought can travel to the farthest star. Through the power of thought, you are capable of grasping the complexities and subtleties of all theories and philosophies, and yet you can go beyond even reason and logic to the direct experience of God. You are original: the pattern of your thoughts and ideas is unique—no one thinks exactly as you do, no one creates in his mind exactly as you do. And yet, in the all-encompassing unity of Spirit, you can know what Socrates knew, what St. Francis knew, what Jesus knew. You can share with all persons that live or have ever lived, the equal and infinite wisdom and love of God. Think of your mind: in all its ways, through the maze of ideas it travels every hour of every day, subtly but surely its leadings are ever toward the highest and the best. As you attune your mind to God, infinite wisdom and understanding open up to you. You discover that there is a universal wholeness of all ideas; the central point of balance is God.

The harmony that exists between nations of the world may at times disintegrate into war, yet eventually the often unconscious tendency of individuals and nations toward peace becomes a conscious tendency. Individuals and groups of individuals begin to work to find ways of resolving conflict. Once again, the ideal of unity is foremost. This cyclic striving for peace is inevitable, for man is really a spiritual being that finds fulfillment only in realizing and expressing in peace and love his spiritual nature. There is a universal unity of all people; the central point of balance is God.

This innate tendency toward wholeness and unity is evident in all of nature. You may wish to reread Pattern Two, Lesson 3, at this time, and think again about the beauty and goodness that is inherent in the world. Only learn to look for it, to reach out for it with your mind and heart, and the spiritual balance of all things will be revealed to you.

Practice Exercise

Become still and focus your thoughts on this diagram of a scale. In order to achieve balance, the line of the scale must be perfectly level. If any weight is added to one side or the other, the equilibrium will be upset instantly. If the horizontal bar is moved to the right or to the left, balance is lost. Only when it is perfectly centered can absolute balance be maintained.

Imagine that your body is like this perfectly balanced scale. Sit with both feet on the floor, spine straight, eyes and shoulders level, arms resting easily at your sides. Think that your body temple is perfectly balanced. You are centered in absolute wholeness, stillness, and peace. Divine order is established in every body system; you are divinely balanced and whole. Put aside your papers now and hold this attitude for a few moments.

If your body tends to sway slightly in resistance, do not be concerned. Only maintain your attitude of balance and affirm softly:

My body is the temple of God, and I am in perfect balance.

As you begin to feel more at ease, a feeling of wholeness and strength increases in every part of your body temple. Your mind tends to focus away from the particular parts of your body and to center in inner stillness. Any discomfort or disorder begins to leave you completely as you reach a sense of oneness and wholeness that transcends physical sensation. Give thanks as you speak the words once again:

My body is the temple of God, and I am in perfect balance.

If there is any disunity or quarrel between you and another person, or if there is confusion or apparent lack in your affairs, bring the image of your spiritual scale to your mind. See that all things are in divine order. Behold that innate spiritual tendency toward unity, wholeness, and balance *active* in your life, and look forward to wonderful results as you affirm joyously:

My life is centered in God, and I am in perfect balance.

Now hold the image of the scale before you again in your mind. Place any fear or worry that you may have on the mental image of the scale, and see that all these negative thoughts are now balanced by the positive ideas of love and peace. Your mind feels lifted almost instantly, for you know that as you remain poised and centered within, all feelings and attitudes of your mind reflect wholeness, balance, and order.

You may want to see the base of the scale as the Christ within, and either side as the physical and mental phases of your being. As you see that both sides of the scale are in absolutely perfect balance, you realize that you are in tune with the source of perfect health, perfect peace. Nothing can upset this divine balance. Hold this idea as you speak these words softly:

My mind is centered in God, and I am in perfect balance.

If you notice that thoughts of other things begin to intrude upon your concentration, see these thoughts on your inner spiritual scale. As you remain centered in God, nothing can upset your equanimity. Give thanks as you silently affirm:

My mind is centered in God, and I am in perfect balance.

Watch your thoughts, record your ideas in your Spiritual Diary, and know that you are centering more and more on God within you. Think of how you are now unfolding. Know that you are reaching that inner point of absolute peace and blessedness, and that you are spiritually strong, healthy, successful, and happy. Give thanks as your growing consciousness of spiritual balance is outpictured in your life!

Pattern Four
Lesson 4

Dear Student:

Have no doubt but that Truth gives freedom, joy, peace, and health. These are the natural and sure outpicturings of the spiritual wholeness you are beginning to experience!

The Christ within you is your unfailing source of harmony and wholeness. Look inward to infinite wisdom for the great idea of unity with God, and know that in this awareness, you are perfectly whole and happy.

A single idea born of wisdom is irresistible. No one can estimate the power for good that is in an idea generated in the center of the home of ideas, the inner man. When an idea comes from that great galaxy of supreme ideas it goes forth in strength and harmony. It is a perfect sphere with no point liable to friction or collision *(Charles Fillmore, Talks on Truth).*

You are lifted by constant love and prayer as you begin this week's study. In this awareness, begin the lesson with a feeling of happiness and expectancy; be receptive to divine ideas, and look forward with faith and joy to wonderful results!

PATTERN FOUR

Learning Wholeness

Lesson 4: Completeness

You have begun to realize that the method of affirmation and denial you have been using can be applied to any challenge in life. But this method of positive thinking is not only a way of regaining your sense of balance when you are ill or disturbed or in trouble; it is not only a method you use when you are in need of a healing in life, but it is a process that is completed in a *constant state of consciousness.*

The secret of healing lies in lifting the

consciousness up by faith into the realm of God perfection, thus clearing the way for God's original perfect healing and blessing work to be done . . . *(Lowell Fillmore, Things to Be Remembered)*.

The use of affirmation and denial is a technique to help lift your consciousness into "the realm of God perfection"—to a state of constant awareness of the infinite goodness of God. A denial need not always be an outright statement, but a kind of mental overcoming of negative appearances; an affirmation need not always be a definite positive statement, but a subtle, inner recognition of Truth. Through the idea of affirmation and denial, you are building a greater consciousness.

You are building a perfect body in your mind; you are building a peaceful, loving attitude; you are building an expectation of good in life. As you continue in this activity, you must watch your thinking very carefully to see that no negative perception impairs this mental image. Let no imperfection of any kind be accepted in your thinking, for how can you be whole if your thinking is not whole? See things as they are, yet see beyond appearances to God, omnipotent good. Let your consciousness expand to encompass the whole of things!

As you grow in this consciousness you attain an attitude of praise; you continually give thanks for this beautiful, perfect body, for this wonderful mind, and for this life of infinite possibility. Praise the health and happiness you idealize. Know that all good is now being made manifest in your life. Turn away from any false appearances, and affirm inwardly with all your mind and heart:

I joyously give thanks that I am whole and perfect, right now.

You can begin to feel the life-giving activity of Spirit bringing your thoughts of perfection into manifestation. God is now manifest in every cell, every idea, every situation. Whatever words or statements you use act as a signal, a preparation for this sense of certainty, this consciousness of completeness.

In this consciousness, you know that God's will for you is perfect wholeness. As you begin to think in accord with this divine will, you *will* healing in all things. You call forth the loving, healing action of God.

You know that God has not given you sickness and weakness and limitation; He has given you health and freedom. Choose these gifts with all your power of will. The affirmations and denials you are using are tools to this end; they express your choice of Truth over false appearances. Through the method of affirmation and denial, you renounce the thought that burdens of ill health or disharmony of any kind are the will of God, and you affirm the truth that that which is changeless good can will only changeless good. You begin to see yourself on your own highest level of expression—that of Spirit, eternal and free. Every apparent obstacle becomes an opportunity for enlightened choice; you choose to give up a false concept or condition, or you choose to overcome it. Often once the choice is made, the obstacle disappears, or its ability to disturb you passes away. You realize that every day is filled with the possibility of overcoming!

Remember how an overcoming feels. Think of physical overcomings: that first morning after a bout with a cold, when you can breathe easily and when you know you are completely well. Think of that deep breath that comes with this realization. Breathe it now—that breath of freedom, of release. Express the feeling that you have in positive words, such as:

I am free of all limitation—I am strong and pure, ready to do great things!

Register the joy of this sensation. Maintain this consciousness of praise and joy. The experience is exhilarating, freeing, for it indicates an underlying unity of all experience.

Out of the duality of good and bad, positive and negative, sickness and health, discord and harmony, emerges a unity that is constant, beyond duality. Your understanding of ultimate good transcends what may seem to be relatively good and right—your mind reaches to encompass the idea that God is far better than you had thought. You may have begun in search of physical healing, mental tranquillity, or harmony in your affairs, and now find that there is a spiritual wholeness that transcends all of these phases of healing.

This truth is your inspiration, yet do not be impatient with yourself or with outer conditions as you work to realize this spiritual wholeness. *Do not be impatient.* Rest in the certainty of God as the all-powerful Healer. Develop a consciousness of completeness, a sureness of God's perfection *at hand.* "Patience is not passive waiting, but active, faithful expectation" *(James A. Decker, Magnificent Decision).* When you develop this quality of patience, you do not give up hope—you give up hopelessness. In this step, believing is completed in being; "I believe" becomes "I am."

Every healing is accomplished through the application of God's principle of wholeness, whether material agents are utilized or not, whether the healing takes place instantaneously or in "God's instant men call years." . . .

Those who traveled a mile to reach and touch Jesus' garment were healed immediately, and so were those who traveled twenty miles. The distance, the time involved, varied for each individual; the healing in each case took place instantaneously.

So it is with our application of the principles of Truth. Sometimes we wait months, or years, for the realization of some cherished desire. Sometimes we grow impatient, or even bitter, when we think that God does not quickly answer our prayers for something that we "really need." Yet the actual demonstration of that for which we pray always takes place instantaneously—when we are ready for it *(James A. Decker, Magnificent Decision).*

Time is finite, yet that wholeness you seek is infinite. Only let your thinking be ready to receive Truth, only be ready to let it be expressed in your life, and any moment is "God's instant." The process of receiving wholeness, of feeling that you are filled with Spirit, completed by God, is really the goal of all religion. In this consciousness, you pass beyond the finite and into the infinite. You leave limitation behind and come into limitless joy and abundance. You overcome self-bondage and reach eternal freedom. You see beyond apparent division to the unity that is divine love.

What does being whole mean in life, in your body, in your mind? That longing for wholeness within you is the love song of all time, of all people in all languages; it is the recognition that to be completed by God is to be whole.

Love, in Divine Mind, is the idea of

universal unity. In expression, love is the power that joins and binds in divine harmony the universe and everything in it *(Charles Fillmore, Christian Healing)*.

Spiritual experience leads you to think thoughts of perfect love and wholeness. When you think these thoughts, you can instantly have a sense of completeness. This sensation is manifest in your physical being as health. This sense of completeness is manifest in your mind as understanding and love; it is manifest in your life as order and peace.

Dwell for a few moments on the qualities you associate with God. You may behold God as perfect health, infinite goodness, wisdom, and love. When you recognize these qualities as the reality in and through all things, you at once begin to see them manifested in your life. It is not only that your increased attention to these qualities makes you more aware of the innate good in your life and affairs; your loving thoughts actually attract to you blessings of vitality, right understanding, and your highest good.

Think of the quality of divine love that you associate with God. This love is infinite, whole, complete. You know in your own experience that when you feel love, you have a sense of completeness, of wholeness. When you love, you actively see the good in people and things. Your thoughts and words of praise bring out the good in others and bring about blessings in your life. The law of healing and happiness is simple—only love. In order to restore wholeness in your body, see the good in it, send love to every part of it. Recognize your body as the temple of the living God. If you want peace of mind and understanding, know that your mind is the channel of expression of your inner Christ self. Lovingly salute this life you live! Praise life!

Have you learned that there is more to life than you had thought? Have you had healings? Then you realize that it is necessary to renounce the thought that "you" are the healing agent. The "you" of appearances, the finite you, does nothing. But that self which is within you, that which is beyond all personality, that which is nameless, ageless, birthless and deathless, is the divine "do-er" in your life. This is the true self of your being; it is self-luminous, eternal.

We are spiritual beings first, before we are mental, emotional, and physical persons. It is this spiritual self that is perfect and whole, always, for it is the self created in the image and likeness of God *(Mary Katherine MacDougall, Healing Now)*.

Do you think that you are suffering? That Christ within is beyond suffering. Do you think that you are weak or ill? That Christ within is untouched by illness, knows no weakness. Do you think that you are unhappy or isolated? That Christ within is eternal happiness and unity. That Christ self within you is dependent on no outer condition whatsoever. It lacks nothing, and is right now absolutely whole and complete. You become one with that self, and the universe is revealed as whole and complete to you when you recognize this reality.

By identifying yourself with the Christ self, you quicken that in you which is correspondent with God. You strengthen that divine connection and clear the channel for all that is good in your life. Just as there is an underlying harmony and perfection in the universe, however things may appear, so also there is an underlying harmony and perfection within you. This is the center of your being, that

243

balance point within you, that inner fullness and completeness of Spirit.

The idea that you are intrinsically whole is not new or foreign or difficult to accept. You cannot read scriptural accounts of healings without a thrill of recognition. You know that healing is more than a possibility; the experience touches on ultimate reality. Healing is undeniable, unchanging, for it is grounded in Truth, it is grounded in you.

That you are spiritually whole and complete is really already known to you. Even when you contradict that inner knowledge, you are aware that you are admitting to a half-truth. You know that an illness cannot be eternal, infinite, but is always somehow separate, transient, false. A physical limitation may affect or influence you, yet it is always less than *you* really are.

The Christ self within you watches over you night and day, without break. In apparent illness or in health, in apparent lack or in abundance, in happiness or unhappiness, it is there, waiting to be realized. There is not a single moment's pause in the constant attention of the Christ in you. Think of this loving intelligence watching over you, abiding within you, strengthening and protecting you in all things. Think of this loving, healing activity with you even when you are asleep, present in every cell and system of your body.

Once you have realized the unlimited healing power within you, you will never again be quite the same. This acceptance and experience of healing brings to you a new sense of wholeness and of the all-sufficiency of God. Immediately give thanks. Thanksgiving is the completion of the process, and the opening of the way for even greater experiences, even more complete oneness with God.

As you give thanks for the wholeness that is now being manifested in your life, it is almost as if you can perceive that still, small voice within you saying to you, "Yes, the healing you seek is already established in Spirit, but do not stop here, for much more awaits you!"

All your life you may have believed that you have been seeking health, but you have been seeking only God. All your life you may have believed that you have been seeking harmonious conditions, but you have been seeking only God. All your life you may have believed that you have been seeking peace of mind, but you have been seeking only God. Come to the realization that God, and God alone, is your goal. With this realization comes the wholeness, the spiritual completeness you seek.

Practice Exercise

Sit relaxed and still, keeping the spine straight. Resolve to experience completeness; resolve to feel oneness with God today. See that all the days of the past and all the days of the future are complete in this present moment. Now is the time to have perfect health, not yesterday or on some future day. Now is the time to be happy; now is the time to know God.

The infinite possibility of life fills *this very moment.* All that you seek is here, in this moment of stillness. Rest in this wonderful idea.

———————

You have a growing sense of oneness. All time is one, all experience is one, and you are one with God and the universe. In God, you are complete.

When you think that you are only a body, or that you are only a mind, you are apart from the universe. When you realize that the divine Self of you is one with God, you are one with all that exists.

As you hold these ideas in mind, let your thoughts flow naturally for several moments. Think of yourself, think of your life; watch the trend of your thoughts.

Although you feel generally inspired about the true nature of yourself, the thought may come to you, "I have a particular physical weakness." At once complete that thought with the truth, "Apparently I have a weakness, but in reality I am whole, healthy, and complete in God; that reality is manifesting in me now!"

Turn your whole attention to this freeing, fulfilling idea. Become still and give thanks that you are whole and complete in God.

If you have the thought, "I have bad habits," or "I feel hurt, resentful, angry, afraid," complete the thought with the truth, "Apparently I am limited in thought and feeling, but in reality I am all-wise, happy, serene, and complete in God; that reality is manifesting in me now!"

247

Turn totally to this idea. Become still and give thanks that you are whole and complete in God.

If any thoughts about negative outer conditions come to your mind, such as, "Life has no meaning; nothing works out right," immediately complete these thoughts with the truth, "Apparently life is chaotic and confusing at times, but in reality, all is in divine order, complete in God; this reality is manifesting now!"

Rest in this thought with all your being. Become still and give thanks that all things are whole and complete in God.

Each day, continue in this exercise in the time you have set aside for your course work. Yet develop the habit of watching your thoughts at other times also. Consciously complete half-truths in your thinking with the Truth you know. Expand your consciousness to encompass the whole of things in every situation, in every experience. You can no longer accept illness or unhappiness for yourself or others, for you see beyond these apparent limitations to the spiritual completeness of all things. You have discovered the secret of wholeness.

It is not necessary to list for you case histories of recovery and healing in mind, body, and affairs through enlightened positive thinking, although truly they are without number. Only follow your innate inclination toward God, and the record you keep in your Spiritual Diary becomes a living case history of your own. Give thanks for the dramatic spiritual unfoldment you have experienced, and for the limitless unfoldment yet to come.

Pattern Five
Lesson 1

Dear Student:

In your life and in your understanding of Truth, things are beginning to "fit together." The experience is somehow like mending a broken cup; none of the pieces can contain a cupful, but when they are carefully glued in place, the cup can be filled. As negative attitudes and disjointed concepts are harmonized by a growing consciousness of the spiritual oneness of all things, life holds immeasurable blessings. Answers and results begin to come to you; ideas and outer conditions begin to fall into place.

But as things begin to fall into place for you, resist formulating any set doctrine. Let general principles of Truth imply particulars.

Change in your ideas about any details—be flexible. However, hold always to basic Truth, for that alone is changeless!

PATTERN FIVE

Learning Abundance

Lesson 1: Recognition

The wholeness you are experiencing is a dynamic demonstration that *God is love.* This is not a static experience, but a realization that is ever growing in magnitude, ever increasing in meaning. You have begun to perceive the nature of divine love. This love ever increases, never lessens; this love is never lacking, but is always full. Dwell on this quality of divine love, contemplate it, grow in it, express it—and all that is in need of healing in your life is perfectly healed, all that is wanting in your life is freely given.

It is good to pause for a moment and know for yourself, "I am loved." Know that you are loved with an everlasting, all-encompassing love. Divine love is sweet beyond words, pure beyond description. Think of this love. Repeat the words "God is love" over and over

251

again until you reach a sense of certainty, a peaceful recognition of this truth. Become still for a moment and let that perfect love pervade your being.

As you contemplate the idea that God is love, your conception of God may change somewhat. Often in the study of religion, God may seem an abstraction, a universal "law" or transcending "principle" that is somehow remote from your life. But when it is realized fully that God is love, this concept must expand. God is abstract, universal, absolute, but God is also Father, close and real.

There may be a slight hesitancy on the part of some to accept this apparently "personal" and thus "limited" attribute of God. However, a "personal" God who is all-loving and dynamic in very immediate ways at the same time retains all the transcendence of absolute law and principle. God is law, but not cold law; He is reality—*living* reality!

There *is* a universal law of healing and prosperity that can be applied in everyday life, there *is* a transcendent, "giving" quality of Divine Mind; yet this changeless principle is active and responsive to you in inexpressibly tender, personal ways. God is infinite, law, principle, yet He is at the same time loving Father—personal and near, the Provider of all good.

The core of this teaching is that God is all, that there is an inherent divine unity in the universe: "There is an all-sufficiency of all things. There is a kingdom of abundance of all things." Further clarification of this idea is given in the works of Charles Fillmore:

God is an intangible essence. Matter is a mental limitation of the divine substance whose vital and inherent character is manifest in all life expression.

God is the formless. God substance lies back of matter and form. It is the basis of all form yet does not enter into any form as a finality. . . . This unfailing resource is always ready to give . . . it must give, for that is its nature *(Charles Fillmore, Dynamics for Living).*

Reread these words and think carefully about the ideas behind them—search for the highest meaning. God is an intangible essence, divine substance, formless, the basis of all form, unfailing resource. In this sense, God's giving, all-providing nature is a changeless law, as God is changeless. Infinite plenty is at hand, available and accessible to all. This is a pleasant, uplifting idea. As you reach an understanding of this idea, you may feel that the map to a hidden treasure has just been placed before you. Yet in another way of explaining the nature of God, Charles Fillmore wrote:

> The Father's desire (law) for us is unlimited good. . . . The Father gives us all that He has and is when we return to the consciousness of His house of plenty *(Charles Fillmore, Dynamics for Living).*

Here is not only the map to the treasure, but the treasure chest brought to you, opened for you, and the treasure placed in your hands. The Father *gives* unlimited good. God is your inexhaustible and ready supply. Out of Him all good flows, in Him all good exists. This law of infinite abundance is not a cold, lifeless metaphysical concept, but a living reality that you can experience. God is law, but law *full of joy.*

He is the treasure, and the Giver of all treasure. For God is also love—boundless, unfailing, gentle, all-forgiving. God is intangible, formless substance, yet God is also loving

Father.

God is one, however variously expressed or known. The truth that right thought, word, and action naturally attract blessings of every kind does not inherently contradict the truth that God, the Father, lovingly gives you *personally* all that is good as fully and freely as you will receive it.

As you recognize God as your loving Father, almost immediately you begin to feel the quality of love kindled in you. The law of infinite abundance becomes real for you through divine love. As you dwell on that divine love, you begin to experience love increasing and unfolding within you. Here is wholeness, peace, beauty, perfection, and abundance expressed. This love is the most powerful attracting force in the universe, for through it you receive healing, you attract right companionship and harmonious conditions, and by it you are prospered. This essential truth emerges out of these ideas:

This divine Substance—call it God, creative energy, or whatever you will—is ever abiding within us, and stands ready to manifest itself in whatever form you and I need or wish to manifest . . . It is the same yesterday, today, and forever. Our desire is the cup that shapes the form of its coming, and our trust—the highest form of faith—sets the time and degree *(H. Emilie Cady, How I Used Truth)*.

Like the loving parent, God holds back nothing from the beloved child, but gives all without qualification, without counting, as generously as the stars are given. You need only look to Him as your infinite, loving supply. Let your thoughts center on this affirmation:

I recognize God, the Father, as the Source of all good.

Resting in this thought, you experience a deep peace, a sense of a "giving," all-providing presence responding to you, enfolding you. Hold to this feeling, rejoice in its nearness to you throughout every moment and circumstance of life, for in this experience you are attuned to absolute healing, understanding, and fulfillment. You recognize, close at hand, the source of all good.

There is that within every human being which is capable of being brought forth into the material, everyday life of any person as the abundance of every good thing that he may desire *(H. Emilie Cady, How I Used Truth)*.

The words "there is that within" indicate that it is necessary at the outset to turn inward and recognize God as the Source of all good. Spiritual understanding always begins with this step. It involves a setting aside of all outer business, a turning away from all previously held notions. This is, in effect, as is every prayer, a recognition of the omnipotence of God. As you think in this way, you are rejecting appearances as final, and turning to the Father within for the highest understanding, knowing that only God can satisfy. Through Him, all good is accomplished. From Him comes all happiness, all healing, all peace, and all supply. In this awareness, affirm joyously:

I recognize God, the Father, as the Source of all good.

The idea of "all good" is a tremendous challenge to the mind, yet through that divine Self of you, this truth is natural and easy. The good that is inherent in every day, in every object, in every individual, is a manifestation of God, the good omnipotent. Think of this; let this great idea uplift and enlighten you.

God is the Source of all good.

Remember that the Source of all good is "within every human being"—not within one more than another. If you have been thinking that because some other person seems to have a greater abundance of health, comfort, happiness, or opportunity, you may be in some way less "worthy" or "capable," let that kind of thinking be transformed now. Such limited concepts will not hold for you; they are out of place with the Truth you know. Go beyond these limits, and rely on God "within every human being which is capable"—*infinitely* capable. This capability includes both ability and capacity. That is, you are divinely able to do unlimited good and to receive with infinite measure, for you are loved with an unlimited, infinite love.

In this sense, you are the eternal coin of the universe that never loses its value. By your very being, you attract all that is good and beautiful and real. If you would have health, happiness, prosperity, you must realize that within you is the matched value of infinite good. Know that all the good you desire is already prepared for you.

You do not "purchase" blessings by your good words or deeds; you draw blessings to you naturally and easily by expressing the infinite loving Spirit that is your true Self. This is not a matter of reward or of exchanging right words and actions for some desired good. How can there be a bargaining between eternity and eternity, between infinite and infinite? Only turn to the Father and receive abundantly. You need not wonder whether or not you "deserve" any desired thing. You do not need to supplicate, to beg, for any needed thing. The loving Father is ready now to give you every blessing.

Remember that the true Self of you is pure, sinless, perfect, heir to all good. That which is limitless and perfect attracts only that which is limitless and perfect. Look out upon infinite good in the world, and look inward upon infinite good in your own being—then you recognize that all you could want is already your own, without cost or limit.

It is a good experience to look up at the sun and see that there is always more sunlight than can be gathered or absorbed or used or taken in. There is more of the world than can be gathered or absorbed or used or taken in. There is more of the sky, more of space, than can be gathered or absorbed or used or taken in. This wonder of abundance is all around you, ready to be recognized.

In your mind, be transported out of the narrow limits of this room, this house, this building; be lifted above the ceiling, be expanded beyond the walls. Stretch over continents and rise into the sky and into space. Feel this infinite abundance; it is measureless without end. Feel the largeness of the universe.

You can hardly think these thoughts without sitting straight and inhaling deeply. Think: "What is this in me that responds so willingly and freely to infinity? Surely I, too, am eternal, limitless, vast beyond measure. All this is without end, and I am without end."

When you look up at the stars and try to count them, you soon lose count and find yourself lost among them somehow. Pause while you are still looking up and be aware of the leadings of your thoughts. What is indicated to you? Do you feel almost transported out of the finite to a sense of the infinite? You cannot really think thoughts of lack and limitation here, for you respond naturally to this greatness with an inner greatness, a "largeness" from within.

You recognize that you have this spiritual quality of largeness when you think of a star shining thousands of light years away and know that somehow it is contained within you; when you look out on a borderless expanse of ocean and know that somehow it is contained within you; when you examine curiously a tree of hundreds of branches, thousands of leaves, myriad veins and patterns on each, and know that somehow all is contained *within you.*

In this mood of thought, you sense the all-encompassing, all-containing nature of God. It is right to feel awe at creation, and it is right to feel awe even at your own awareness. It is right to feel *love,* for this all-pervading largeness of the universe, of all things great and small, is love abundantly expressed. It is fullness, it is sufficient in itself, without envy or lack or limitation. It is enough and more than enough.

Truly, God is love—boundless, limitless love. This abundant love is knowable as infinite supply; the key to experiencing abundance in life is in the recognition that the abundance of God is everywhere.

This universe is a boundless expression of the infinite love of God. It is inexhaustible as the love of God, it is unfailing, endless as the love of God. Yet through your perfect inner Self you span the universe, you reach outward and inward to receive infinite good, for you recognize that God Himself is abundance, everywhere present.

Practice Exercise

Give thanks as you begin to work with this exercise that within you are infinite wisdom and limitless capacity to receive your good. Whatever material possessions, prosperous conditions, or spiritual insight you need are already prepared for you; you have only to recognize God as the Source of all good, and let your mind be open to receive His abundance.

Become still and think of God, your loving Father, who is omnipresent, transcending all appearances, yet present and real in all things.

His love enfolds you now and stands ready at this moment to pour out to you infinite good.

As you hold to this idea, affirm with inner assurance:

God, the Father, is the Source of all good.

To guide your thinking to full recognition of this truth, make a list in your Spiritual Diary of all the good things and conditions you now enjoy in your life. Add to this list often during the month as your awareness of the good around you increases. Be specific in your list; try to include as many of the blessings in your life as you can. You may want to list home, possessions, car, food, clothing, money; and you may wish to expand this list to include friendships, marriage, children, your individual freedom, good health, abilities, your work, entertainment, and so on.

As you record these blessings, pause and consciously bless each item on your list. Close your eyes after each item you write and as you think of it with praise and thanksgiving, affirm:

I recognize God, the Father, as the Source of this good.

263

It may be difficult not to resist this affirmation with the limiting thought that you yourself bought, produced, or brought to yourself this particular blessing completely on your own, or else that it came from some other source than God. But the beginning of a consciousness of abundance is in the full recognition that God, God alone, is the ultimate Source of all good. Bless yourself and others as "secondary sources" of your good, and know that in these ways God's infinite love and supply is wonderfully expressed.

You may find as you think of these things that an attitude of joy and satisfaction begins to prevail in your mind. As you look at the list of your good, when you begin to feel almost the same wonder and gladness that you feel when you lose count of stars, or marvel at the expanse of nature, you are truly reaching a consciousness of abundance.

As you turn to God as the Source of all that is good, you begin to delight in the world, in life itself, even more fully than before. The pen or pencil you write with, the comfortable chair you sit in, the sound of the rain, a smile, can all be recognized as blessings that fill every day.

Do not be impatient in what seems like merely "counting your blessings," for in this activity you reach the awareness that your life has a spiritual "largeness" about it that reflects the largeness of the universe. The loving presence of God fills every day with infinite abundance, and all things are enough and more than enough.

Your recognition that God is the underlying principle in the universe, that He is embodied in all that exists, becomes real and fulfilling as you realize that you are *personally* blessed. You are the beloved child of an infinite and loving Father, and you are unfolding in wonderful ways! Let every day be a celebration of His abundance everywhere present, and let your thinking be attuned to receive infinite good. In joy and expectation, affirm:

God is the Source of all good.

Pattern Five
Lesson 2

Dear Student:

As you undertake this week's lesson, let this simple statement of Truth harmonize and clarify your thinking:

There is but one Presence and one Power in the universe, God the good Omnipotent, and God is love!

This is all you really need. The rest, the endless questions about life and death, cause and effect, do not really fill the moment. But the simple Truth that *God is, and God is love* is enough in itself to answer all questions ultimately, and to satisfy all desires.

God is love.

These three words are enough to form the basis of all religions, and yet may be the only essential teaching. God is love—such infinite love that is all-providing, all-fulfilling. Hold to this Truth—be filled with it!

PATTERN FIVE

Learning Abundance

Lesson 2: Readiness to Receive

In order to learn the nature of abundance in life, continually expand your thinking to a sense of the "largeness" of the universe. Be ever aware of the infinite abundance of good that is now manifest all around you. Keep the quality of being able to be transported, lifted to a wider, fuller perception of things. Cultivate this quality, and be ready to experience joy and wonder at all times. As when you look up to see a flock of birds rushing overhead, you are transported, you take in more of life for a moment. Then when you look down again to what is immediately around you, you look with eyes more open, joyous, awakened, and more expectant of good. Something happens in your thinking so that you perceive an abundant supply, a continuing wealth and freedom beyond appearances.

Let your mind flow with the idea of an endless wheat field, the measureless sands of the ocean floor, the numberless waves of the ocean itself, the countless stars, the freedom of the winds. Here is true prosperity! Think in this way, and you have the key to the riches of the universe.

As this sense of spiritual largeness and all-sufficiency awakens in you, you realize that the Christ within you is greater than any negative appearance. You then know for yourself:

The Christ in me overcomes appearances— my needs are filled and my life overflows with good!

You know that the Christ within overcomes obstacles and needs of every kind. Keeping your thoughts lifted to this level, you do not give any power to apparent limitations; you hold before you the spiritual reality and know that it is right now coming into manifestation. Knowing that your needs *are* filled, you open the way for an overflowing of good in your life. Take the words of the affirmation above silently—make up your mind to demonstrate this Truth!

———

Determine not to entertain thoughts that

are limiting, but fill your mind with ideas of abundance. Guard your speech so that only ideas of success, prosperity, and plenty are expressed. In this higher consciousness, lack is overcome, overtaken, covered, filled, and overflowed with good. If a need appears in your life, know *more* than the need, know *abundance*. Think beyond emptiness to fullness, beyond questions to answers, beyond unhappiness to happiness. Look forward at all times to the realization of your good, and be ready *at any moment* to claim it boldly and gladly.

If you find yourself thinking or speaking negatively about yourself, your life conditions, your future, or about others, deny the limiting thoughts; give appearances no power over you or over others, and affirm the positive Truth. You may want to choose a word, such as *plenty, supply,* or *abundance* to keep in mind. When you are faced with apparent lack, center on this word—dwell on the ideas it represents to you. Say the word silently whenever the need seems greatest, and use the word often in your speech. Bring your thoughts up to its level. Know ideas of abundance, and they will manifest!

Begin now. The thought that says, "I am sick," "I am in want," "I am discouraged," "I am in trouble," is a harmful thought. Throw it out. Replace it with the thought, "God means me to be well and happy and to have abundance." This creative thought will immediately begin to build its substance, its realization *(William A. Clough, How to Claim Your Good)*.

Again and again it is necessary to peel away the outgrown concepts about yourself and the life you want to have. Do not give time and energy to destructive speaking and thinking. Give up any stifling or defeating thoughts and habits. Instead, give your time and energy to ideas and expressions of success and plenty.

In light of the Truth you have experienced, you cannot really believe that anything less than the highest and the best is prepared for you. Therefore, it is necessary to consider whether you want and expect everything to continue in the same way, or if you are ready and willing to accept positive change. However pleasant or productive life is, can you not see beyond to even greater good, even fuller opportunity to know and express God?

Be transported by that thought! Be ready now to accept positive change—be ready to realize a greater abundance of good. Think what it would be like to be told that you had just inherited a vast fortune, or to discover the answer to a once troubling problem, to find all at once that an old misunderstanding is transformed into a harmonious relationship, or to realize your true spiritual treasure fully and dynamically right now. Accept the idea, not with fear or disbelief, but with joyful thanks. Think that wonderful things are now happening to you! Let faith overcome any fear. Only the mind can limit your good; therefore, let your mind be opened to *unlimited* good. Still all other thoughts for a moment, and accept this idea:

I am empty of fear and limitation; I am filled with faith and the prospering love of God!

As you repeat the words aloud and then silently hold the thought, you realize that no problem or need can be the center of your life. The light of eternal peace, perfect love, and infinite supply is the center of your life! Will to accept this idea freely and fully, and

271

let fear and limitation be banished from your mind. The prospering love of God fills you, uplifts you, and makes the way to your good clear and straight. You are ready to claim the success, prosperity, and fulfillment that is yours by divine birthright. Give thanks that there is nothing to stand in the way of the expression of your Christ nature!

By holding ideas of Truth, and by using affirmations, you are not calling into being that which does not exist. You are becoming receptive to the positive *reality* and preparing yourself as a channel for its expression. If you should begin to think that by directing your mind and by using denials and affirmations, you are somehow "controlling" the power of good so that you may use it as you please to bring about whatever results you think are best, you fail to perceive the object of spiritual development. The object of spiritual development is the realization that God is the supreme *Doer*—God is the one Power and Presence in the universe. Inspired by this Truth, you would never want His perfect expression to be limited in any way by selfish desire. Having attained that realization, you become one with infinite wisdom and joy.

When you are truly empty of fear and limitation and filled with faith and the prospering love of God, wonderful things begin to happen! Often when some particular good you have been seeking does come to you, a "bonus" or some unlooked-for, unthought-of good comes with it. Perhaps you will receive not only what you had been seeking but something more besides, or you may receive more of the needed thing that you had even thought to ask, or perhaps something will come about for you that is better in every way than what you had sought. The law of prosperity is not only that you receive what you ask, for if you make your mind ready to receive your *highest good*, whatever it may be and however it may be manifest to you, then you will receive abundance to overflowing!

There is one sure progress and evolution in the universe, and that is in the individual's realization of God as the one Presence and Power in the universe. All outer progress and change is really an outpicturing of that inner growth. If you seek God realization sincerely and earnestly, that inner "progress" has a force and direction that is stronger than any appearance. Seek to know God with all your mind and heart and you will be bountifully provided for in every detail. As you realize that the very nature of God is boundless love, unlimited joy, infinite peace and wisdom and abundant supply, these divine ideas are naturally outpictured in your life. Seek God always as the highest, the purest, the fullest, and you will experience Him!

Practice Exercise

As you begin this exercise each day this month, start with an attitude of boldness. Take a deep breath, and feel that you are inhaling abundant strength, wisdom, and faith. Be bold to claim the infinite good that is prepared for you; be bold to grasp the nature of abundance; be bold to know God!

Become physically and mentally still and receptive as you consciously empty your mind of all negative thoughts about your life, or the state of your health or prosperity. Repeat the affirmation below, first aloud and then silently to yourself, as you let the Truth of it fill your consciousness:

I am empty of fear and limitation: I am filled with faith and the prospering love of God!

274

If any thoughts about lack or apparent obstacles of any kind are persistent in your mind, transform these thoughts of negative appearances with overcoming love as you use the statement again:

I am empty of fear about this apparent limitation; I am filled with faith and the prospering love of God!

As you clear out of your thinking all doubt, all concepts that seem to block your good from you, make of your mind a cup—a readiness and an openness to receive your highest good.

Do not permit worry or speculation about how exactly the good you desire can come to you get in the way of your realization. Merely be confident and ready to receive fully.

Be bold to experience the infilling of the prospering love of God! Be totally receptive now to the sensation of spiritual fullness.

This experience may be somehow like a deep, invigorating inhalation of air, or like the quick flooding of a stream, or like a cup being filled to overbrimming, or like suddenly looking up to see the sky filled with stars. Patiently and expectantly watch for the feeling once more.

275

Register in your mind the sensation of spiritual infilling; write about it in your Spiritual Diary. Try to capture in words something of the experiences you have in working with this exercise as you keep your notes; for in thinking of it, in recalling it, and in striving to understand it, you will find that the experience grows in depth and meaning.

Remember, the spiritual sense of abundance that is the basis of a consciousness of prosperity is waiting to be experienced by you at all times and in all circumstances. Give thanks as you affirm:

I am filled with the prospering love of God!

This new awareness brings with it a sense of inexpressible joy, fullness, completeness, wholeness, and all-sufficiency. You know that you are unfolding spiritually! Be boldly expectant of the blessings that are even now, at this moment, manifesting in your life as you declare:

The Christ in me overcomes appearances— my needs are filled and my life overflows with good!

Pattern Five

Lesson 3

Dear Student:

Let your mind flow with the eternal message, "God is love, God is love, God is love!" You are discovering that this simple yet profound truth is not to be set aside as you leave your place of study each day; it is not apart from or out of place in daily living. For the truth that God is love unifies all religion, all philosophy. Moreover, it unifies religious thought with that which seems secular. God is love—in this idea your need for health is not out of place. Your search for happiness, your dream of peace, your hope for success, your wish for prosperity, are not out of place here.

Within this simple truth lie infinite implications for good. Growing in the consciousness

277

of God as love and all-sufficiency, you find that your capacity to be healed, to be happy, and to be prospered is ever growing. The facets of your identity and the fragments of your experience are brought into focus, into unity with God, and your life fills with His goodness!

PATTERN FIVE

Learning Abundance

Lesson 3: Receiving Abundantly

The attitude that makes greatness in life, the secret of abundance, is to know that God is the source of all good and to be both content and patient in that awareness, yet also quick to respond as a ready channel for good. When this attitude is fully expressed in your life, nothing whatsoever can stand in the way of your good. Know that the loving and giving law of abundance is now at work in and through all persons and situations. Think not of limitations and lack, but of that never-failing law of abundance. Neither fear nor doubt can hold you below the level of the good you seek. Rejoice in that freedom!

No person or circumstance can possibly keep your good from you once you recognize that God and God alone is the ultimate provider of all fulfillment, ever ready to pour out to you abundance of every good thing. That realization is expressed through you both as a patient willingness to receive rightly at the right time and in the right way, and as a dynamic, energetic readiness to act, work, and do whatever is right for you to do.

The key to all wealth is already in your hands; the key to all understanding, all joy, is already in your hands. Let your thoughts, words, and actions express confidence in success and faith in the abundance that is yours. Get the idea that in life, no time is wasted, no good is ever lost or taken away from you. In every moment, working or resting, awake or asleep, you are *successful*. See yourself as radiating the Christ within in rich ideas and rich experiences *now*.

Like the king who had forgotten for a time his birthright of power and plenty, discover again your own divine kingship. Seek in these words (and in everything in life) reminders of your spiritual royalty! Think what it is like to be a king, to have sovereignty; think of perfect authority, power, security, and freedom. You know that, in reality, you are a king— you have only to realize that the true self of you is the highest authority, unlimited power, perfect peace and security, and absolute freedom. Turn within now and contemplate that inner Christ self.

The Christ self of you is indisputable and all-wise authority. It is that still, small voice, that perfect inner "knowing," that is ever available to you. Affirm for yourself:

I am abundantly wise in Christ.

The power of the Christ within you is unlimited and irresistible. When you exercise the power of the Christ self to turn your thoughts toward positive Truth, your whole being responds. Your life and affairs are irresistibly turned toward positive change. Affirm for yourself:

I am abundantly powerful in Christ.

Think of the security of the Christ. Here is the serenity, peace, protection, and contentment you seek. Let these thoughts fill your mind. No temporary outer appearance can touch this inner security. Affirm for yourself:

I am abundantly secure in Christ.

Think of the freedom of the Christ. This is

perfect self-confidence, ability to express, un-limited capacity, self-reliance, and great joy. Center on the Christ within and you are free of all limitations. Affirm for yourself:

I am abundantly free in Christ.

No matter what outer conditions may seem to indicate, overcome negation by identifying yourself with the positive qualities of the Christ. Think of that inner, perfect Christ self as you say "I" in these statements:

I am wisdom.
I am power.
I am security.
I am freedom.
I am health.
I am harmony.
I am abundance.

Peacefully and confidently rest in this Truth; become still and inwardly take the statements above. Be determined, yet patient to receive the fullest meaning of the words. Take a long moment to feel the meaning, for all time is abundantly yours.

The infinite abundance of the universe belongs to that Christ within you. That is the very essence of confidence, peace, satisfaction, all-sufficiency. Know with all your mind and heart that the Christ is the very nature of yourself and of all persons. In reality, you are rich in all good, and all people are rich in all good.

Your own source is everyone's source. You cannot really think of God, the source of all good, as open to you yet closed to someone else. Knowing that infinite good is open to all, opens the way for your spiritual development and frees others to express the highest within them.

As you realize the true nature of abundance, more and more often you stop the sentence that begins, "I am afraid . . . " even before it is quite formed. You let fear pass out of your thinking as you feel courage and patient faith rise up in your mind and heart. The understanding of abundance is developing in you as a *heroic* attitude. As you think of heroes throughout literature and history, and recognize in them a quality of boldness and insight that oversteps limited appearances, you feel this quality coming to fullness in you.

Knowing and living the Truth you have found, you *are* heroic, even when doing apparently unimportant work. More and more you seek out, become receptive to, and boldly accept opportunities to work in positive, constructive ways whether on a great or a small scale. More and more you dare to live a happy and prosperous life—more and more you accept your spiritual royalty.

In order to claim your spiritual heritage, you must decide for yourself: "Which is the ultimate Truth; which is the reality I live by? Is it appearance, or is it God, the good omnipotent?" The answer is already within you.

Realizing that God, the good, is the ultimate Truth and reality, you see at once that life is not purposeless, but full of purpose. Life is not boring and empty, but delightful and challenging. If you have ever believed that there were real reasons for your problems, turn within and know that there are infinitely greater reasons for the overcoming of all problems. Let this heroic attitude strengthen and uplift you. Be inspired to do all that needs to be done by you.

Work as an outer activity follows "work" in the mind. Work on these ideas, use affirmations, watch your thoughts, and creative, prospering work will open up to you. Move into whatever work is at hand with zeal and enthusiasm. However seemingly insignificant or tiresome or difficult the work may seem at first, do it in a loving, giving spirit, and only good will be forthcoming.

As you work, think of abundance. There is abundant good to be realized through every activity, and you have abundant energy and ability to realize it! As you work, sleep, eat, walk, and read these words, you are achieving abundantly; you are attaining your highest good.

As you work, think, *"God is now being expressed through me."* There is no difference between the simple duties you may perform and all great undertakings when every activity is seen as the expression of the Christ self. Lift your attention from appearances and center your mind on the Christ within. This is the focal point of God within you. This is the good you desire above all else; here is the Giver and the gift as well.

. . . when you continue to think about God as your real supply, everything in your mind begins to awaken and to contact the divine substance, and as you mold it in your consciousness, ideas begin to come which will connect you

284

with the visible manifestation. You first get the ideas in consciousness direct from their divine source, and then you begin to demonstrate in the outer *(Charles Fillmore, Prosperity)*.

Persevere in visualizing God's good regardless of surrounding appearances. It is easy to recognize God's abundant good when you watch the sun rise or set, or a summer downpour or a field of spring flowers. But perhaps the best time to learn the nature of abundance is right in the midst of apparent lack. In these instances, "continue to think about God as your real supply"—turn to the divine Source of all good, and receive abundantly.

It is a good practice to go back to the suggestions in Pattern Two concerning the ability to appreciate beauty everywhere, even in the seemingly ordinary. This same ability is necessary in developing a consciousness of plenty. As you hold to positive ideas, you know with certainty that any negative elements of failure or hindrance are now being transformed into positive realities of victory and release.

Often just when outer appearances seem locked to any positive change, if you can see abundant prosperity, happiness, and healing as already true and real in Spirit, then in perfect timing and in perfect ways right solutions to every difficulty become apparent. If you become impatient, only work harder to think and express divine ideas of supply, order, and freedom. Abundance is now manifesting for you—*it must manifest.*

Ideas have an inevitable effect on appearances, for it is the irresistible tendency of ideas to be expressed, to be formed into being. If you would have your whole life lifted now, reach to the highest thoughts. Think of the real spiritual treasure that is the Source of all good. Give thanks, for that treasure is your own.

Do you not feel completed, nourished, comforted, and renewed in an inner way by the ideas of Truth you are thinking? Ideas outpictured as art, scientific discovery, literature, and good words of every kind are satisfying. As you think such ideas as:

I am rich in health, peace, and plenty!

Life, love, wisdom, and power are mine in abundance!

you begin to feel satisfied. It is not that you are settling for appearances, or that you are complacent about the words of the affirmation, but that you can actually feel the ideas expressed working into manifestation.

These ideas seem easy and simple, yet it is the central, ongoing work of the universe to reach a constant awareness of divine ideas. Certainly learning abundance is a dynamic activity that requires work. Yet the realization you are seeking is also found in a quiet, seemingly passive "knowing." As in all things, it is the role of the aspirant to be in a sense active, yet also passive; to be in a sense impatient to know God, yet ever patient to know God.

You have been working with various exercises in positive thinking, with many illustrations and affirmations of Truth, yet at the same time that you are "working" in these ways, you are increasingly aware that the Father within you is at work. The moment comes in outer activity as well as in inner activity when you feel that the work of the personal you is taken up by God. Instantly you feel at peace; you are satisfied. Quietly and patiently, you know at firsthand:

God now abundantly provides!

Even as you are experiencing this feeling of fullness, you perceive that not only are your material needs being met abundantly, but that something else is happening to you. This peace, this satisfaction, overflows material fulfillment; it is the overflow that exceeds specific desires and spills into every area of life. This is the spiritual experience of God as abundant good. This experience is always at hand, however outer conditions may change, whatever new challenges may arise. Through this realization, you receive not only an expanded capacity to experience prosperity and harmony in life, but moreover, you receive a heightened and intensified spiritual understanding. God now abundantly provides!

Practice Exercise

As you sit quietly, assume the stillness and control, yet readiness for action, of a soldier at attention. You have accepted a heroic challenge; you are involved in a great work!

Recognize all personal desires as subtle indications of the inner desire to know God. As you work for fulfillment of various desires, realize that you are really working toward the realization of God. More and more you are awakening to the idea that all work is, in reality, part of a universal work. You are involved in a universal inward working with divine ideas as well as an outworking of divine expression.

Try to combine these two attitudes in your thinking: an alertness and readiness for positive action, and a patient, confident letting-go. Speak these words:

I am alert and ready to claim my birthright of happiness, freedom, and prosperity!

Now pause for a moment and rest in this thought:

I let God do His perfect work.

In the first statement, you are affirming that all good is divinely yours. All qualities of the Christ self, such as wisdom, power, security, freedom, health, harmony, and abundance, you hereby appropriate for yourself. You *are* these qualities, for your Christ self is the very essence of all good.

Let go completely of any limiting thoughts about yourself or your life. There is nothing that can limit you or keep your good from you. See yourself as rich, wise, and radiant with Christ ideas. Keep the idea of abundant good that is divinely yours foremost in your mind. Affirm joyously:

289

I behold myself well, happy, prosperous, and free!

Register your feelings now; write about how you feel in your Spiritual Diary. Surely, "work" is involved in gaining the realization of God as abundant good. Yet at the same time, you begin to feel released and satisfied. You begin to relinquish any feelings of work or struggle. It is natural to breathe deeply and easily now. Softly, then silently, affirm:

I let God do His perfect work.

The personal you is out of the way now, for you let God do His perfect work of establishing divine order, harmony, peace, and fulfillment within you and all around you. You know that whatever you have need of is now a present reality in your life. All that may have seemed empty is now filled; all that may have seemed wanting is now received.

A wonderful awareness of wholeness, fullness, and satisfaction follows the recognition that God is now at work in your life. You freely claim the divine ideas of abundant good that are your spiritual heritage, and you freely let them be expressed in all that you do. You and all that come in contact with you are prospered and blessed a thousandfold!

Give thanks, for you abide in riches, you live in abundance! Be happy, for in all things, God does His perfect work through you. Give thanks that you are unfolding in the awareness of divine abundance, everywhere present. Keep record of your experiences in your Spiritual Diary, for they are treasures; they represent the gift of self-realization that the loving Father extends to you at every moment. Receive that gift gladly and freely now!

Pattern Five

Lesson 4

Dear Student:

Resting in God's perfect love, you are healed and happy. The time involved in this realization, the outer circumstances that come into play, the "details" in this healing, fulfilling experience are diminished by the all-important Truth that God is love—unifying, eternal, infinite love.

As you begin this new period of study, work and live in the awareness that you are loved. You are loved by students of Truth everywhere; you are united with all mankind in the all-pervading love of God; you are God's beloved child, to whom all good is given and all Truth is revealed.

While your consciousness of the loving

nature of God increases every day, every day there is more good to experience. Give thanks, for with every thought of praise and thanksgiving, your capacity to receive increases, and you are infinitely blessed.

Realizing that God is love, you know that you are spiritually whole and that you are heir to abundant good. There is no lack, for God is your all-in-all.

PATTERN FIVE

Learning Abundance

Lesson 4: Right Desire

You know that in reality, God is good everywhere present. As you recognize this Truth, you begin to rely on your spiritual resources. You begin to rely on the Christ within to direct all of your desires rightly and attract to you your highest good. The Christ within is infinite and cannot be attached to finite things; yet dwell on the Christ self, and the spiritual power that is released in your life will be expressed in abundance of every good thing. It is not for the acquisition of possessions that you seek spiritual understanding;

yet in seeking spiritual understanding above all else, you will attract all that you could ever need in "good measure, pressed down, shaken together, running over . . ." *(Luke 6:38)*.

You cannot be satisfied with less than infinite good, for God within you and back of each longing and desire is infinite. It is not possible to limit this spiritual power to expression only in a particular possession or outer condition. Therefore, in a spiritual sense, desire *all* good, not just portions of good. Although you see the sun reflected in pools of water, in the lake, the ocean, the river, you know that these reflections are not the sun itself. Seek not the manifestation, but God who is manifest as all good.

The needs and desires of every day have always changed with time and events; they are changing now, and they will always change. But God, the Source of all good, is truly changeless. God is manifest as the answers to every need—He alone is the true object of all desire. Follow your inner desire to know God—seek Him above all else, and all that is needed in your life will be supplied. Realize at every point that He and He alone is the

Source of all you could want.

He is the light of every pleasure, the warmth of every comfort, the beauty and value latent in every possession. The moment you seek anything for its own superficial sake, you cannot really be satisfied, for it is the quality of the Christ within to transport the mind beyond limited appearances to the ever greater freedom of spiritual experience. Therefore, do not let your mind become too attached to transient things, but only to God.

In order to be really free and happy, get the realization that what you seek is really infinite good—inexhaustible, eternal, transcendent. The secret of true prosperity is to enjoy the abundance of life without attempting to hoard it; to use without destroying, to appreciate without attachment. You know that if you value possessions or prestige for their own sake, you have nothing. Yet worship God as the one infinite good that shines through all things, and everything is yours. You take for your own the best, the sweetest, the purest in life, and you take it freely and joyously, yet leave plenty all around you. Behold God in and through all things. Behold the world as the beautiful and abundant

295

expression of God.

The joy of God, the wealth of spiritual experience, is unlimited. Things change, desires change, but God is changeless good. You may no longer take joy in a childhood plaything, but God is undiminished joy—that which cannot grow stale or be lost or worn out. Through that joy, the beauty and riches of the world are revealed to you.

✓The "prosperity consciousness" that you seek is not only the awareness that more money or possessions or more health or understanding can be gained through right thinking; the prosperity consciousness that you seek is the full and constant awareness that God is unlimited, all-sufficient, ever-accessible good. If an individual thinks that the real source of his supply is his employer, he thinks he is cut off from his good if he loses his job. But once he realizes that God is the ultimate Source of all good, he is confident and receptive to the new and fuller channels of supply that are opening up to him.

✓Your loving Father is like a "wish-fulfilling tree"—an inexhaustible, ever creative and infinitely abundant Source of good. There is more here than you could ever ask for. What will you ask the wish-fulfilling tree? Will you ask for some commodity? Very well, you can have that. Will you ask for pleasanter circumstances? Very well, you can have them. Will you ask for healing of some irritation? Very well, it shall be healed. But it is as if God within lovingly says: "But is that all? Here is eternal happiness, boundless love, infinite wisdom, perfect peace. Beloved, only open your hands and receive this treasure!"

Is it wholeness that you want? God is wholeness.

Is it love that you want? God is love.

Is it supply that you want? God is supply.

Is it peace that you want? God is peace.

Is it wisdom that you want? God is wisdom.

Is it life that you want? God is life.

God and God alone is the ultimate fulfillment of all desires. Look to that divine Source always—think of it, keep in tune with divine ideas, and receive abundantly.

You perceive that in and through all other desires, the supreme desire and leading of your life is to realize your oneness with God in all things. If anxiety interferes with that realization, determine to be rid of the anxiety and to attain a peaceful, receptive state of mind. If physical discomfort or weakness seems to interfere with that realization, determine to be rid of sickness and to be strong and healthy. If material need or lack of any kind seem to interfere with that realization for you, determine to be rid of the problem—determine to be prosperous. The goal is God-realization; therefore, do away with any thought or circumstance that seems to hamper you in this. Deny whatever seems to limit you, and see beyond appearances to peace, vitality, and abundant supply. Seek to realize God in all things, and above all else. For in peace of mind and harmony of affairs, God is manifest; in health and vitality, God is manifest; in comfort and plenty, God is manifest. Never think that God is these manifestations and nothing more, but never forget that God is dramatically revealed in these ways.

Do not condemn your desires, for although your thinking may be in error at times, desire itself is really the urging toward greater expression of your Christ nature. Give thanks for this inner leading and follow it to its highest demonstration. Let go of guilt or self-condemnation concerning your desires.

Always be honest with yourself, yet keep the courage to change. Become still now, and keeping your desires in mind, center on these words:

Thank You, God, that this or something better is now manifesting for me!

As you repeat this affirmation, close your eyes and see all your desires purified and rightly directed. Place your trust in infinite wisdom, and know that God is now active in your desires and in your affairs to bring about the right outworking of your highest good.

When you consciously examine your desires, there is a tendency to judge things according to their *use;* to consider whether they are *practical* or not. But the idea of use is relevant to more than the material plane of life. It is also right to judge according to "spiritual use"—that is, how the object or experience may teach, suggest, or indicate the spiritual reality. From this standpoint, it is not necessary to separate the "spiritual" from the "practical." Religion is limited if it is interpreted only to bring prosperity or health in a transitory, superficial way. But religion is truly great when it sees the everyday duties and achievements as suggestive of *spiritual* attainment. In this sense, religion may be immanently "practical." And yet, even if a man worships God only for the rewards that thinking about God will naturally bring, he will at least *think about God.* The real and lasting reward becomes his even if he did not seek it for its own sake in the beginning. The joys of spiritual understanding will soon overshadow other concerns in his mind, and eventually he will attain the true sense of abundance far beyond his original aim. It is as if the man comes into an orchard to steal away only one apple, and is told that the entire orchard really belongs to him. As he realizes the true value of his legacy, his satisfaction and fulfillment are much greater than he could have imagined before.

As you let your desires be purified by right understanding, you no longer want a particular possession for itself alone, but you seek God in and through all things. It is not a person or a specific condition that you want, but God in and through all persons and all conditions. Then you can have the cream of life, the wheat without the chaff, the delight without the burden of attachment. Possessions wear out or are lost, but God pervading all things is changeless. People may not always express the highest within them, but God within them is all-loving and all-wise. Conditions may seem chaotic or destructive, but God (whose presence is everywhere in every time and place) is perfect peace and order waiting to be demonstrated!

Practice Exercise

Take time now to become peaceful and still in your place of study. The one true Source of all the good you could ever desire is close now. The very air is filled with the presence of God—divine substance, rich beyond words with all good. Think of the very air as the presence of God. It surrounds you, enfolds you, embraces you now. Taste of it, drink of it deeply and fully as you breathe. Close your eyes and let yourself become completely immersed in the abundance of God.

All that He has in store for you is right here, right now, ready for your claiming. It is the very Being of God—shining everywhere in all places and through all people. It shines through you!

God, the good omnipotent, is here now. Your active recognition of His abundant nature—immediate, nearer than breath or life itself—charges the atmosphere around you with light, life, abundance.

Think of the desires you have concerning your life now—however insignificant or magnificent they may be, however trivial you may think they are, or however vast and idealistic, hold them lovingly in mind. Even as desires come into your mind now, they are suffused with the light of God's substance, dynamic and responsive in this very place, this very room.

As you sit straight, yet comfortably poised, both feet on the floor, head erect, cup your hands before you on your lap, as if in readiness to receive. And you *are* ready to receive—to receive a wonderful gift, a present from God.

Let your mind become open and receptive as the cupping of your hands suggests; become ready in mind and heart to receive divine substance. Let a sense of gladness fill your consciousness, for here is the essence of all good, the essence of dreams fulfilled.

Feel that this divine essence, this beingness of God Himself, this substance is flowing into your cupped hands like clear, fresh, sparkling water. It is filling your hands now and over-flowing, continuously filling them, filling them, filling them. Feel it flowing over your fingers and down the backs of your hands. It is the very love of God, the very wisdom of God, the very nature of God, flowing out to you unceasingly.

The cup of your hands is like the shaping of desire in your mind and heart; God is ready to fill each desire with good, and at the same instant to cleanse and purify your thinking and feeling. You are receiving now—even more than you can hold!

The good that flows to you now is ever new, ever refreshing, and it renews and re-freshes you continually—without pause. You have only to keep open to its eternal infilling and cleansing. Know for yourself:

The love of God, the divine substance of God, purifies and fulfills me now and forever.

Your loving Father is your infinite, eternal Source. Your good can never be shut off from you, never taken away or used up, for it is an eternal spring. God readily and freely fulfills your desires—even the desire that is always there behind every desire—the longing for God-realization. In this awareness, lovingly affirm:

The infilling of divine love satisfies me now, and I am grateful and happy!

Let your heart fill with the acknowledgment, *"Thank You, Father!"* Maintain an attitude of joy and receptivity as you record your experiences in working with this exercise in your Spiritual Diary. Wonderful ideas are flowing out to you now!

Keep the feeling of spiritual fullness, of transcendent joy. You are eternally blessed! You are unfolding!

Printed U.S.A. 127-F-7913-25C-10-85